third edition

Cradle to
Career
in California

a resource guide for parents

Lianne Richelieu-Boren

Kendall Hunt
publishing company

Kendall Hunt
p u b l i s h i n g   c o m p a n y

www.kendallhunt.com
Send all inquiries to:
4050 Westmark Drive
Dubuque, IA 52004-1840

Previously Published by Mascot Books

This book is dedicated to my parents, Robert Richelieu and Carlene Richelieu. Through their never-ending love and devotion, they both instilled in my brother and I the incredible value of pursuing a fulfilling career through any higher education path of our choice.

This book is also dedicated to my two beautiful children, Sean and Kaiya. My utmost dream as your mom is that you find an educational path that leads to a career that gives you as much personal fulfillment and satisfaction as I have. Please follow your dreams, young ones, wherever they take you. I love you to the moon and back.

Contents

Preface

Cradle to Career in California is a resource guide written specifically for parents of children in grades K–12. Parents with children who will be the first in their family to attend college or parents whose children will be following generations of family college graduates will all benefit from the information and advice provided.

Simplified checklists, roadmaps, and worksheets are used to help parents plan and stay on track with all facets of college preparation from as early as elementary school through the first year of college.

Cradle to Career in California explains how college preparation begins in elementary school, walking parents through several activities to help their children succeed from kindergarten through the first year of college. One important goal of this book is to explain the often confusing college jargon and acronyms in simple, basic, and friendly language. Chapter topics covered include preparation starting in elementary and middle school, career exploration, choosing a college major, the higher education options available in California, freshmen and transfer admissions requirements, financial aid and scholarships, college decision-making, and a final chapter on helping parents and students survive the first year of college. The appendix section includes useful tools such as a high school checklist for parents by grade level, a senior year financial aid checklist, a student time management tool, and a college decision-making tool.

Preparing for college admission can be an overwhelming process but parents, you are not alone. Instead of worrying that you missed an important step, you, as a parent, can use this book as a resource tool to relax and even enjoy the college preparation roller coaster ride.

Acknowledgments

The third edition of this book would have not been possible without the generous support of Kelly Salter and the Board of Directors at The McConnell Foundation. I also wish to acknowledge the generous support from the University of California, Davis campus. I am tremendously grateful for the contributions from several team members working for the UC Davis College Opportunity Programs department. Finally, this important work could not continue without the dedication and tireless efforts of team members from the new College OPTIONS Inc., non-profit organization. The important work of this organization is supported by the volunteer efforts of seven community leaders who are serving as this organization's founding Board of Directors.

"This book is a great resource for gaining a thorough understanding of the multi-faceted language related to achieving the training and education necessary for today's careers. I am confident that parents who take the time to read the chapters that are relevant to their child's life stage will be able to glean useful information to help guide them through the long, sometimes complicated educational paths that occur from pre-kindergarten through high school. Three cheers for the **Cradle to Career** *in California."*

Joe Wyse, Superintendent/President,
Shasta-Tehama-Trinity Joint Community College District

"This non-judgmental handbook provides guidance for what every parent wants—a better life for their child. The author clearly steps through the large and small details, making this book a useful, hands-on guide for any parent and the student they are supporting.

Even the most dedicated counselors and teachers can forget how confusing the process, jargon and hidden rules of the college planning process can be. This book would be an asset to any educator's collection to remind them of the benefit of sharing useful information that all parents need to know.

As the author notes 'there is no greater investment' that each, and all, of us can make in your future than to ensure no capable mind misses the opportunity to pursue their passion, and the educational path best suited for them to attain it."

Marian Murphy-Shaw,
Siskiyou County Office of Education

"Until now, I felt I had a better guide to using my microwave oven than to my child's higher education and career path. Lianne Richelieu-Boren has written a book Californians desperately need, at a time when the questions facing parents and students at every level have become more and more complicated.

Cradle to Career in California *is clearly written and organized like a good user manual or travel guide—you'll get the most out of it if you read all the way through, but that's absolutely not necessary. Is your middle-schooler falling behind and acting detached and angry? Check the section on bullying.*

Overwhelmed by the language of early high school years? Skip straight to the clear, concise explanation of SATs, ACTs, and A through G requirements. Wondering whether to call your child's college professor directly? There's an answer for that (it's no, don't and never, by the way).

This is a hands-on, practical guide that doesn't confine itself to any one aspect of a child's successful path, and accounts for all the complexity of that crazy and individual path we all take to adulthood. Of all the things you'll invest in along the way, this guide is going to give you the greatest return on investment. I highly recommend it and will keep my own dog-eared copy handy for years to come."

Silas Lyons,
Editor Redding Record Searchlight

"From my perspective as someone who has toiled in these vineyards for the last 40 years, I believe that this book will provide parents with an easy-to-follow and well-designed guide to their role in promoting, supporting, and encouraging their children to succeed in the educational enterprise as a path to a fulfilling life. Moreover, this book's ultimate outcome is that California's future will be richer, more prosperous, and more enriched by virtue of the diversity of its residents who have earned a college education, gained the skills that this state needs to compete in the global economy, and are prepared to lead California in the future."

Penny Edgert,
UC Office of the President

"Cradle to Career in California is a must-read for parents, students, educational leaders, principals, and teachers. This book is a fabulous 'How to,' addressing all the elements crucial for students to be prepared for CHOICE in their futures. It is a roadmap to be easily followed by families and educators alike, providing guidance, suggestions, and examples along the way. Every family and classroom should have a copy!"

Cheryl Olson, Assistant Superintendent,
Enterprise Elementary School District

"Cradle to Career in California is well worth reading whether you know most of the information being shared or if it is all new to you. I am a college graduate and was amazed to find the cross reference of salaries to jobs, the new careers available and the information about what careers will have more or less competition in years to come. Your child should pursue an education that fits their passion, but the information concerning the many options available today is worth the read."

Laurie Baker,
Chief Executive Officer of the Redding Convention & Visitors Bureau

"Cradle to Career in California is an invaluable guidebook for any parent with goals for their children. It illuminates a long term pathway towards higher education, which in turn helps break down social barriers and provide future directions toward financial success, social mobility, and the means and appreciation for giving back to the community."

Kerry Caranci, CEO,
Shasta Regional Community Foundation

About the Author

Lianne Richelieu holds a Bachelor's of Arts degree in Psychology and Education from the University of California, Davis, and a Master's of Science degree in Career Counseling from California State University, Sacramento. She worked for the University of California, Davis, in the field of educational equity and access for over thirty years. Ms. Richelieu has devoted her entire career to working with first-generation college-bound students via the federal TRIO programs of Upward Bound, Educational Talent Search, and Gear Up. In 2003 she became the founding Executive Director of the College OPTIONS Program, an educational outreach center serving thousands of students and families located in far Northern California. Ms. Richelieu currently serves as the CEO of the new 501c3, non-profit organization, College OPTIONS Inc. She works and lives with her family in Redding, California.

Introduction

I believe that my most important role in this lifetime is that of a parent. In this role, my goal is to serve as a positive guide during my children's journey to adulthood. It is my strongest wish that my son and daughter's journeys will include some form of higher education after high school, but that will ultimately be their decision, not mine. Another important role of mine is that of an educator, working with college-bound youth. I have loved this profession since I started working as a college student with the UC Davis Upward Bound Program in 1984. This work has truly been a life calling, and one that I cherish every day.

My role as a parent and an educator did not fully collide until my oldest child, my son, started attending middle school. Suddenly I had several of my friends and relatives asking me questions about the college-going process. I soon realized that all parents have questions about this process, regardless of whether or not they attended higher education institutions themselves. In short, the college-going process has become so complicated in the past several years that no one has all of the answers anymore.

It is through this discovery and the amazing work of my wonderful colleagues that this book came to be. It is my sincerest hope that this book can help all parents, from every walk of life, to understand the college-going process that is ahead for their child.

As a parent, you hope for a fulfilling and prosperous future for your children and will do everything you can to help them become successful adults. However, how do we, as parents, know how to guide our children to find that lifetime of health and happiness that we so desperately want for them?

First, and foremost, you are to be applauded for reading this book. While we do not claim that it will have all of the answers, we hope this resource can at least guide you in your efforts to plan and prepare for your children's educational and career future. As you will learn in Chapter 1, a successful life for your children growing up today will absolutely need to include some form of education after high school. What do you need to do today to prepare your children for their future? What do you need to know? The answer is: A LOT! This book is designed to help you find many of the answers to your questions and provide information that will help you guide your children through the confusing maze of the educational choices ahead of them. It is our goal to explain each and every step in a language that parents can understand and not in "educator speak," which most of us with careers in education are guilty of using.

Three Key Messages

The first key message of this book is that every student preparing for the job market of the future will absolutely need some form of higher education and/or training after high school. There are many paths to higher education whether your child's educational goal is a nine-month certificate in wind energy technology, or a master's degree in social work.

The second key message of this book is that the word "college" has come to mean many different things. The term "college" includes four-year public and private universities offering bachelor's and graduate degrees. It also includes community colleges offering two-year degrees and certificates, and career/technical training schools specializing in short-term training for specific occupations, and even military training programs. For the purposes of this book, we will refer to ALL education after high school as "college." We are incredibly fortunate to have so many educational choices available in the state of California and in the nation.

The final key message of this book is that one college or career pathway does not fit all students. Your challenge as a parent is to help your child learn about and discover his or her unique self. Our goal is to assist you in helping your child to discover unique talents, interests, and strengths that will lead him or her to pursue an educational program after high school that fits with his or her interests and strengths. This strategy is the best way to obtain a successful career that will give your child a lifetime of personal and financial fulfillment.

**For ease of reading, we will be alternating the pronouns "his" and "her" from chapter to chapter.

Chapter 1

Why Go to College?

"The foundation of every state is the education of its youth"—Diogenes

---

Many parents want to know: why is going to college so important? After all, a college education is expensive and can take many years to complete, with no real guarantee of a job afterward. Despite the expense and time involved, however, your child and society as a whole will benefit from your child's education after high school.

A COLLEGE EDUCATION BENEFITS THE STATE, THE NATION, AND SOCIETY

Numerous research studies over the past five years have pointed to the importance of higher education for the economic benefit of the family, the state of California, and the nation.

- In 2012, a Pew Research Center study found that 40 percent of 18- to 31-year-olds who had earned only a high school degree or less were still living at their parent's home. The percentage of adults who chose to live at home with their parents after receiving a college degree was only 18 percent.

- According to the Pathways to Prosperity study by the Harvard Graduate School of Education, 47 million new jobs will be created nationwide by 2018. However, about two-thirds of these jobs will require some sort of education beyond high school. This means that by 2018, our country will need millions of students to obtain college degrees—but our country is projected to fall short of the needed number of college degrees by at least 3 million degrees (From: Help Wanted: Projections of Jobs and Education Requirements 2010, Center on Education and the Workforce, Georgetown University.)

- California is on track to face a similar shortage of college graduates. To meet the state's productivity demands estimated for 2025, it is estimated that the state will be short by 2.3 million college graduates. (From: The Road Ahead: Higher education, California's promise, and our future economy, California Competes, 2012, Rockefeller Philanthropy Advisors, Inc.)

- More than one-third of California's families are considered low-income, earning less than $45,397 a year for a family of four in 2013. California is first in the nation for the number of adults without a high school diploma or equivalent. Even worse, more than one out of ten adults over twenty-four years of age in California has less than a ninth grade education. (From: Working Hard, Left Behind: Education as a pathway from poverty to prosperity for working Californians, 2013, The Campaign for College Opportunity.)

- Although there have been hundreds of programs and much state legislation aimed at addressing the education and income gap in California, the fact is there remains a huge educational disparity within our state. This disparity creates a terribly uneven playing field for the millions of California children from low-income families. Research has shown clearly that low-income, first-generation students whose parents never went to college are at an automatic disadvantage compared to their peers whose parents experienced the college enrollment process before them. Studies show that children from middle- to high-income families are eight times more likely to earn a college degree than their low-income counterparts. (Harvard, Pathways to Prosperity)

- Even though there are thousands of "free" financial aid dollars available to lower-income students, many of these families are unfamiliar with the information needed to navigate and access these critical resources that are necessary for a smooth entry into our higher education systems.

THE PERSONAL BENEFITS OF ATTENDING COLLEGE

If your child pursues a higher education, a few of the personal benefits he will most likely receive include:

- An increased chance for financial security.
- Better employment options over a lifetime.
- Improved health.
- Personal fulfillment.

The ever-increasing cost of a college education makes it critical to understand the financial benefits your child will receive upon his completion of a higher education. Therefore, the first section of this chapter will focus on the potential financial benefits for a future college graduate.

Financial Security

Experts who have researched the job salaries of college graduates have concluded that college graduates who possess a minimum of a bachelor's degree on average earn $26,038 more per year than those who only possess a high school diploma (U.S. Census 2014). The following chart shows the differences in annual salaries by education level attained.

Because college graduates can expect to earn a salary almost double that of high school graduates, your child will be much better off financially if he completes some form of higher education after high school. Keep in mind that this difference in salary will increase and compound over your child's lifetime.

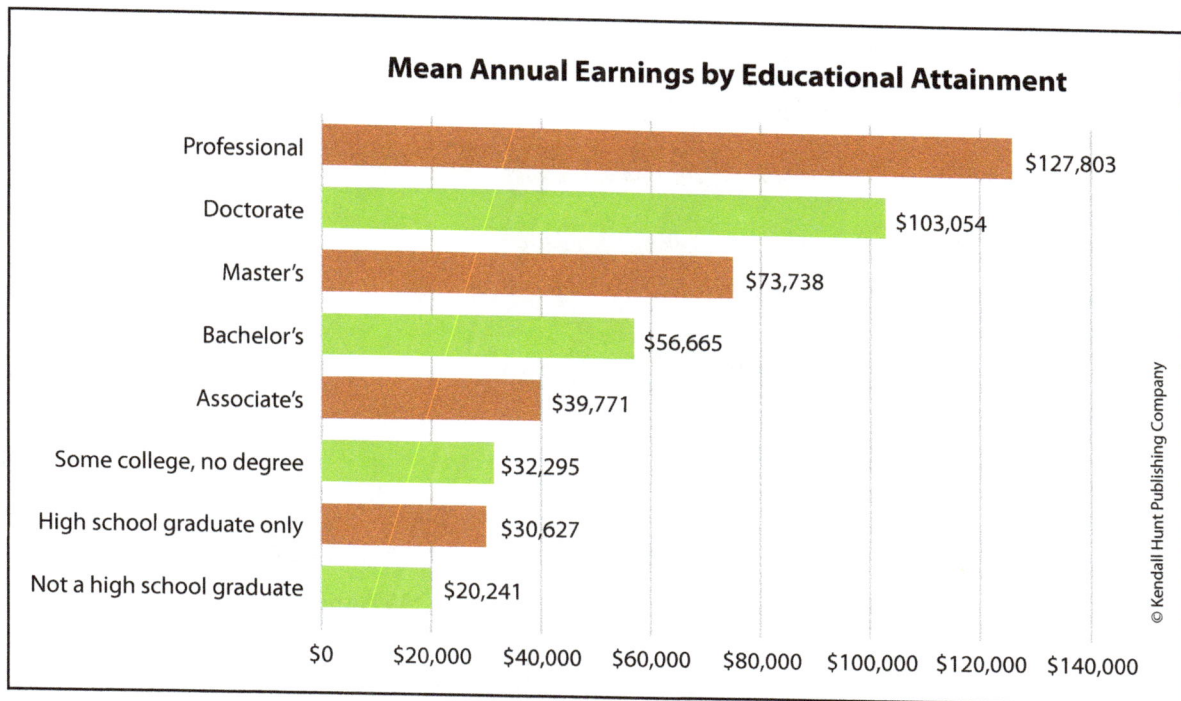

Mean Annual Earnings by Educational Attainment

Educational Attainment	Mean Annual Earnings
Professional	$127,803
Doctorate	$103,054
Master's	$73,738
Bachelor's	$56,665
Associate's	$39,771
Some college, no degree	$32,295
High school graduate only	$30,627
Not a high school graduate	$20,241

© Kendall Hunt Publishing Company

Figure 1   Mean Annual Earnings by Educational Attainment. Source: U.S. Census Bureau.

Employment Opportunities in the Future

The world has changed in just the past twenty to thirty years. The manufacturing, mining, lumber, and other skilled labor force jobs have vanished and in their place are thousands of new jobs that have been created in the fields of technology, information, and research. Most of these new jobs require some form of higher education. Of the 47 million new American jobs expected by 2018, more than 63 percent will require some type of education beyond high school graduation (Harvard, Pathways to Prosperity).

Research also confirms that the higher level of education your child obtains, the less likely he will be unemployed as an adult. The chart below confirms this point utilizing the 2013 U.S. nationwide unemployment rates by educational level (U.S. Department of Labor 2013).

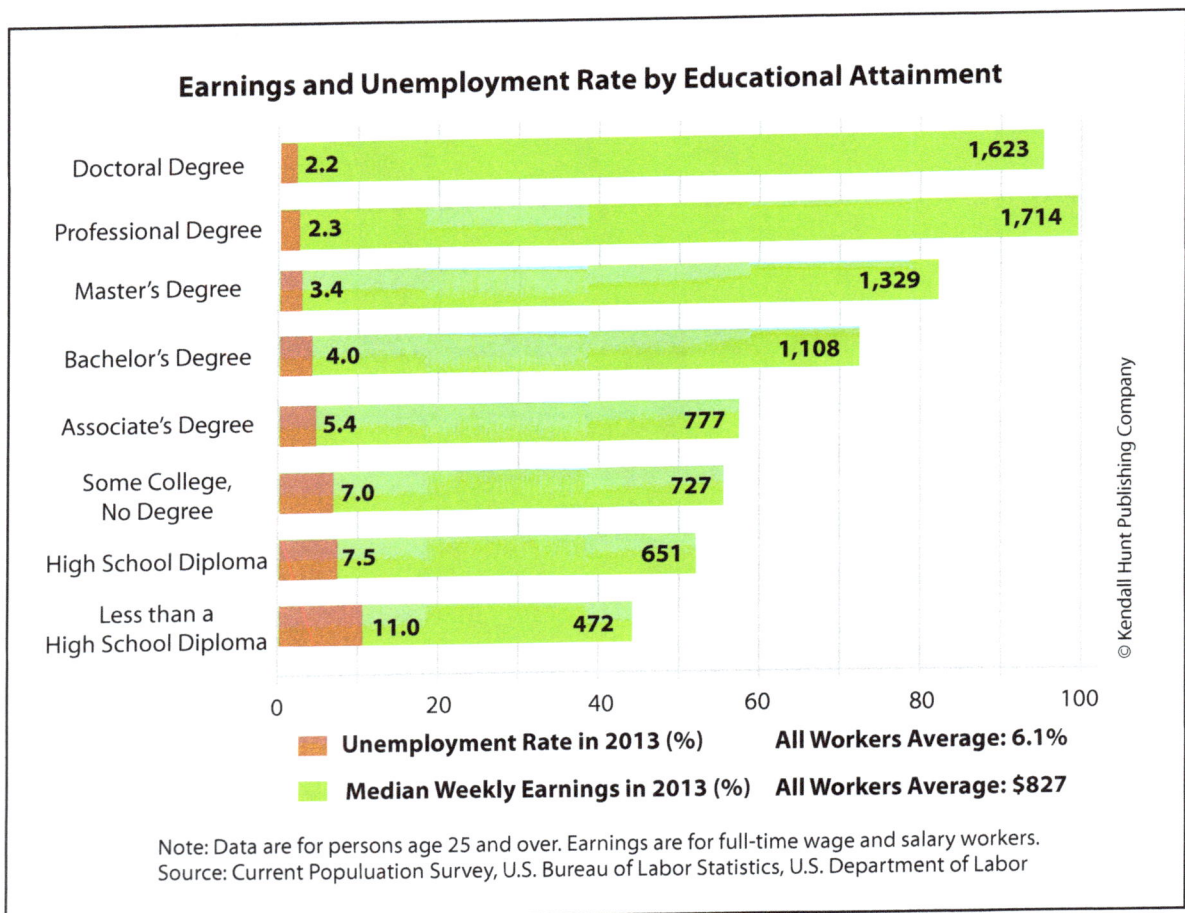

Earnings and Unemployment Rate by Educational Attainment

Educational Attainment	Unemployment Rate in 2013 (%)	Median Weekly Earnings in 2013 ($)
Doctoral Degree	2.2	1,623
Professional Degree	2.3	1,714
Master's Degree	3.4	1,329
Bachelor's Degree	4.0	1,108
Associate's Degree	5.4	777
Some College, No Degree	7.0	727
High School Diploma	7.5	651
Less than a High School Diploma	11.0	472

Unemployment Rate in 2013 (%) — All Workers Average: 6.1%
Median Weekly Earnings in 2013 (%) — All Workers Average: $827

© Kendall Hunt Publishing Company

Note: Data are for persons age 25 and over. Earnings are for full-time wage and salary workers.
Source: Current Population Survey, U.S. Bureau of Labor Statistics, U.S. Department of Labor

Figure 2 Earnings and Unemployment Rates by Educational Attainment.

Increased Income with Jobs That Do Not Traditionally Require a College Degree

Research also shows that individuals who attend at least some college after high school increase their overall earnings potential throughout the course of their lifetimes. The Center on Education and the Workforce at Georgetown University study (Help Wanted) points out that the value of college is not merely that it's necessary for many good jobs, like doctor, teacher, scientist, or corporate executive. A college degree also often lifts people's earnings in occupations that do not require a degree, such as construction worker, day care worker, plumber, and secretary. For example, if your child obtained a job in a middle-skilled profession such as construction, he could earn almost $20,000 a year more if he worked in the same job but also held a four- year college degree.

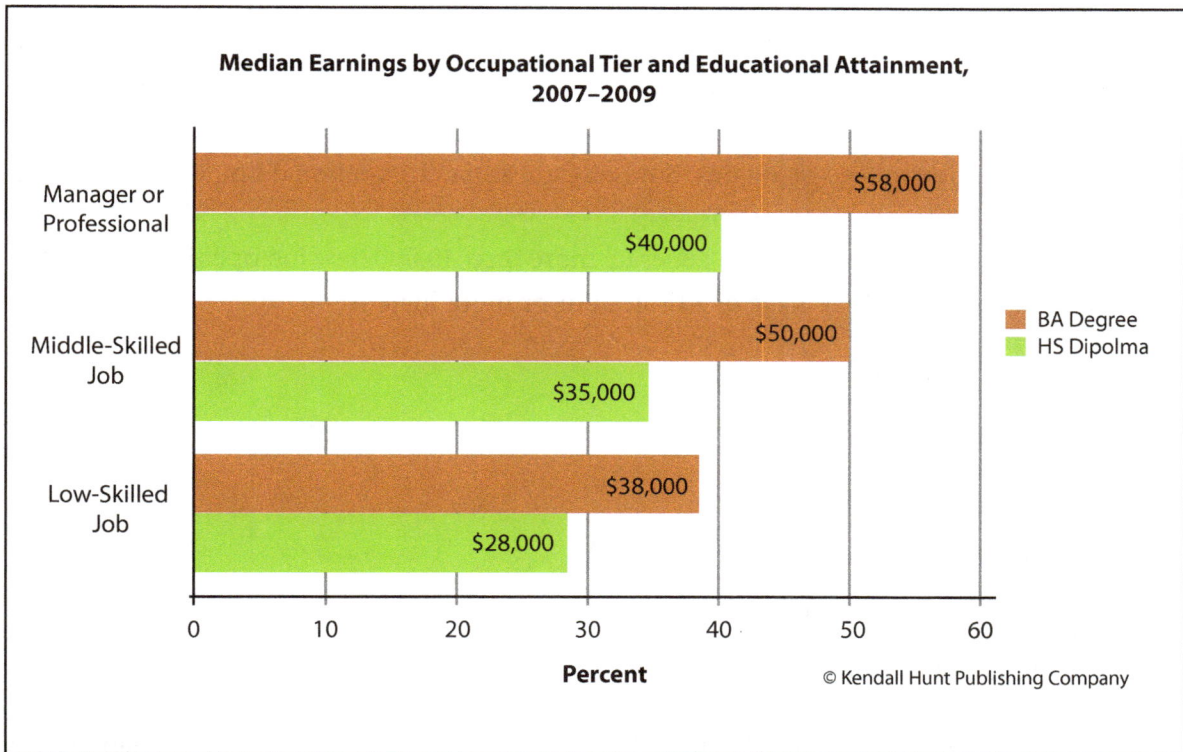

Median Earnings by Occupational Tier and Educational Attainment, 2007–2009

	BA Degree	HS Diploma
Manager or Professional	$58,000	$40,000
Middle-Skilled Job	$50,000	$35,000
Low-Skilled Job	$38,000	$28,000

Percent

© Kendall Hunt Publishing Company

Figure 3   Median Earnings by Occupational Tier and Educational Attainment, 2007–2009
Adapted from Center on Education and the Workforce, Georgetown University.

Increased Number of "Middle-Skill" Job Openings

What parents should also be aware of is that of the millions of new jobs expected by 2018, a substantial share of them will be in "middle-skill" occupations that will require only a training certificate or associate degree. Examples include careers in nursing, health technology, commercial construction, manufacturing, and natural resources. Twenty-seven percent of individuals working within these fields actually earned more than the average four-year college graduate in 2014. For example, the demand for middle-skilled professionals is exploding in the nation's fastest growing industry of healthcare, which added more than a half-million jobs during the Great Recession and is expected to grow by more than 1 million jobs by 2018. These are all solid, well-paying jobs that do not require a four-year college degree, but DO require some form of training after high school (Pathways to Prosperity).

Job Growth

California alone is expected to add almost 2.6 million new jobs to reach a total of over 18.5 million jobs in the state by 2025. It is predicted that the period from 2015 to 2025 will be characterized by widespread job growth as the economy recovers from the recent recession. Job areas that were slowed by the recession are now projected to expand and provide new job opportunities for college graduates (Source: California Occupational Employment Projections 2010–2020).

Occupations that are expected to generate more than 40,000 new job openings in California and pay a median hourly wage of $25 an hour or more include:

- General operations managers
- Registered nurses
- Accountants and auditors
- Sales representatives
- First-line supervisors of office
- Administrative office workers

By achieving some level of education beyond high school, your child will dramatically increase his opportunities to be hired for and paid well in one of these new jobs.

The following table lists the top twenty-five jobs projected for growth in California over the next ten years, sorted by the educational degree needed.

Occupational Title	Degree/Years	Med. Annual Salary
Loan Officers	HS + Certificate	$67,494
Medical Secretaries	HS + Certificate	$34,480
Pharmacy Technicians/Sales	HS + Certificate	$38,285
Security and Fire Alarm Systems Installers	HS + Certificate	$43,881
EMTs and Paramedics	HS + Certificate	$31,578
HVAC and Refrigeration Mechanics and Installers	HS + Certificate	$51,356
Diagnostic Medical Sonographers	Associate (Two-Year)	$83,540
Veterinary Technologists and Technicians	Associate	$34,876
Cost Estimators	Bachelor's	$67,087
Credit Analysts	Bachelor's	$71,275
Database /Operations Administrators	Bachelor's	$80,523
Health Professionals	Bachelor's	$49,891
Interpreters and Translators	Bachelor's	$45,510
Logisticians	Bachelor's	$78,861
Market Research Analysts and Marketing Specialists	Bachelor's	$68,104
Network and Computer Systems Administrators	Bachelor's	$81,358
Accountants/Personal Financial Advisors	Bachelor's	$61,610
Software Developers, Applications	Bachelor's	$104,691
Software Developers, Systems Software	Bachelor's	$114,795
Training and Development Specialists	Bachelor's	$64,471
Healthcare Social Workers	Master's	$60,777
Marriage and Family Therapists	Master's	$66,311
Biochemists and Biophysicists	Doctoral	$81,515
Medical Scientists, except Epidemiologists	Doctoral	$83,430
Pharmacists	Doctoral	$130,563

Table 1   Expected Job Growth in California, 2015–2025.
Source: California Occupational Employment Projections, 2010–2020.

The following table lists the top twenty jobs projected for growth in the nation through 2017 and *which require a bachelor's degree or higher* (Economic Modeling Specialists International MSI 2013).

Description	2013 Jobs	2017 Jobs	Change	% Change	Med. Hourly Earnings	Education Level
Biomedical Engineers	21,273	26,076	4,803	23%	$41.66	Bachelor's
Interpreters & Translators	70,490	81,563	11,073	16%	$22.39	Bachelor's
Meeting, Convention, and Event Planners	87,337	100,429	13,092	15%	$22.56	Bachelor's
Med. Scientists, Non-Epidemiologists	100,742	115,936	15,194	15%	$36.95	Doctoral
Market Research Analysts and Marketing Specialists	438,851	499,740	60,889	14%	$29.10	Bachelor's
Petroleum Engineers	40,853	46,369	5,516	14%	$63.67	Bachelor's
Biochemists and Biophysicists	28,536	32,225	3,689	13%	$39.36	Doctoral
Audiologists	12,914	14,586	1,672	13%	$33.48	Professional
Physical Therapists	208,096	235,802	27,706	13%	$37.93	Professional
Marriage & Family Therapists	42,238	47,743	5,505	13%	$22.35	Master's
Health Educators	58,626	65,676	7,050	12%	$24.15	Bachelor's
Mental Health Counselors	131,331	147,117	15,786	12%	$19.26	Master's
Healthcare Social Workers	152,383	170,104	17,721	12%	$24.19	Master's
Occupational Therapists	113,478	126,801	13,323	12%	$36.55	Master's
Athletic Trainers	21,593	23,933	2,340	11%	$20.39	Bachelor's
Training and Development Specialists	231,960	256,355	24,395	11%	$27.14	Bachelor's
Logisticians	128,825	142,502	13,677	11%	$35.08	Bachelor's
Database Administrators	119,833	133,089	13,256	11%	$37.39	Bachelor's
Geoscientists, Except Hydrologists and Geographers	39,114	43,380	4,266	11%	$46.53	Bachelor's
Software Developers, Systems Software	420,109	468,400	48,291	11%	$47.64	Bachelor's

Table 2 Fastest-Growing Occupations Requiring Bachelor's or Higher*
*At least 1,000 jobs added.

Value of Lifetime of Earnings

It is often surprising for many parents to realize that obtaining a four-year college education means that their child will end up earning more than $1.2 million more over the course of their lifetime than someone who completes only a high school diploma. The following chart illustrates the difference in earnings over a lifetime by level of education completed.

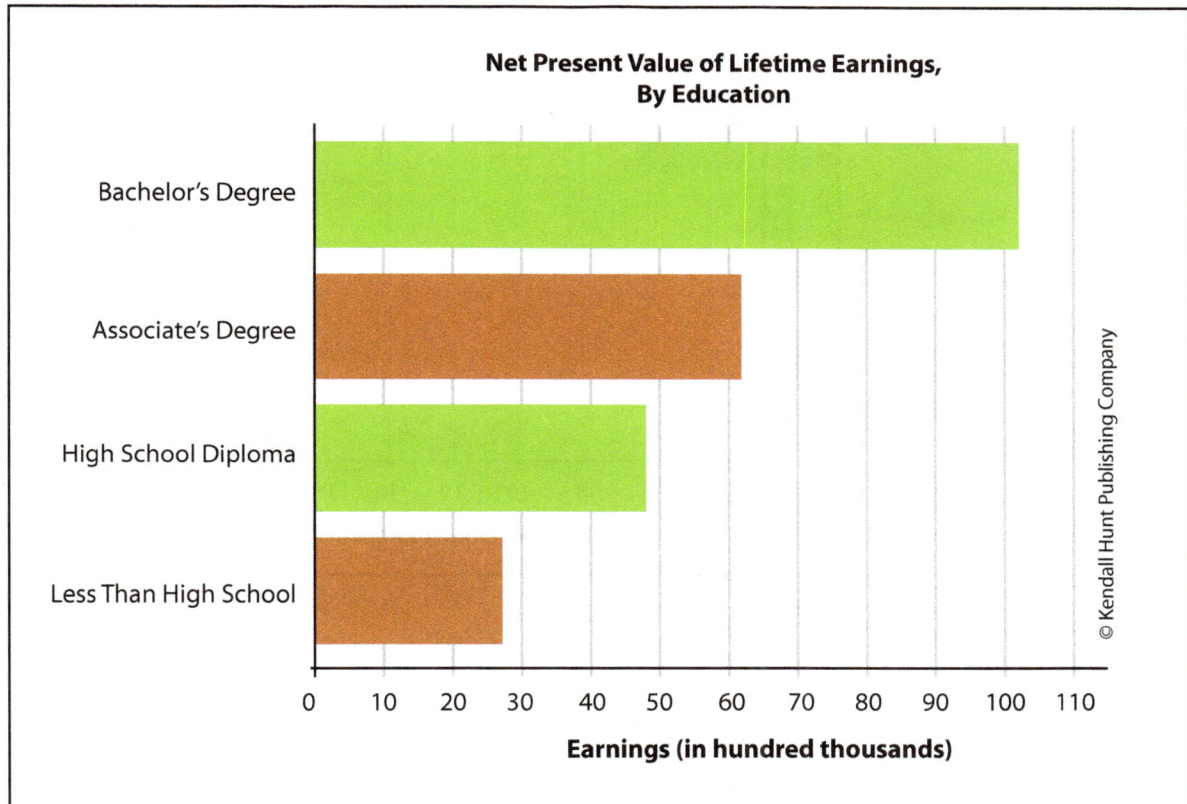

Net Present Value of Lifetime Earnings, By Education

Education	Earnings (in hundred thousands)
Bachelor's Degree	~102
Associate's Degree	~61
High School Diploma	~48
Less Than High School	~27

© Kendall Hunt Publishing Company

Figure 4   Net Present Value of Lifetime Earnings, by Education Level.
(Adapted from Mark Kantrowitz, "The Financial Value of a Higher Education," Journal of Student Financial Aid, NASFAA 2014).

Lifetime Return on Investment

Considering the data available, when making the decision of whether—and where—to send your child to college, you should consider those years of higher education as a lifetime investment in your child's future.

In 2010, The Hamilton Project found that the cost of college tuition in recent decades has delivered an annual rate of return of more than 15 percent. For stocks, the historical rate of return is only 7 percent and only 1 percent for owning a home, as shown in the following chart. This makes college still an incredibly profitable investment of your family's resources.

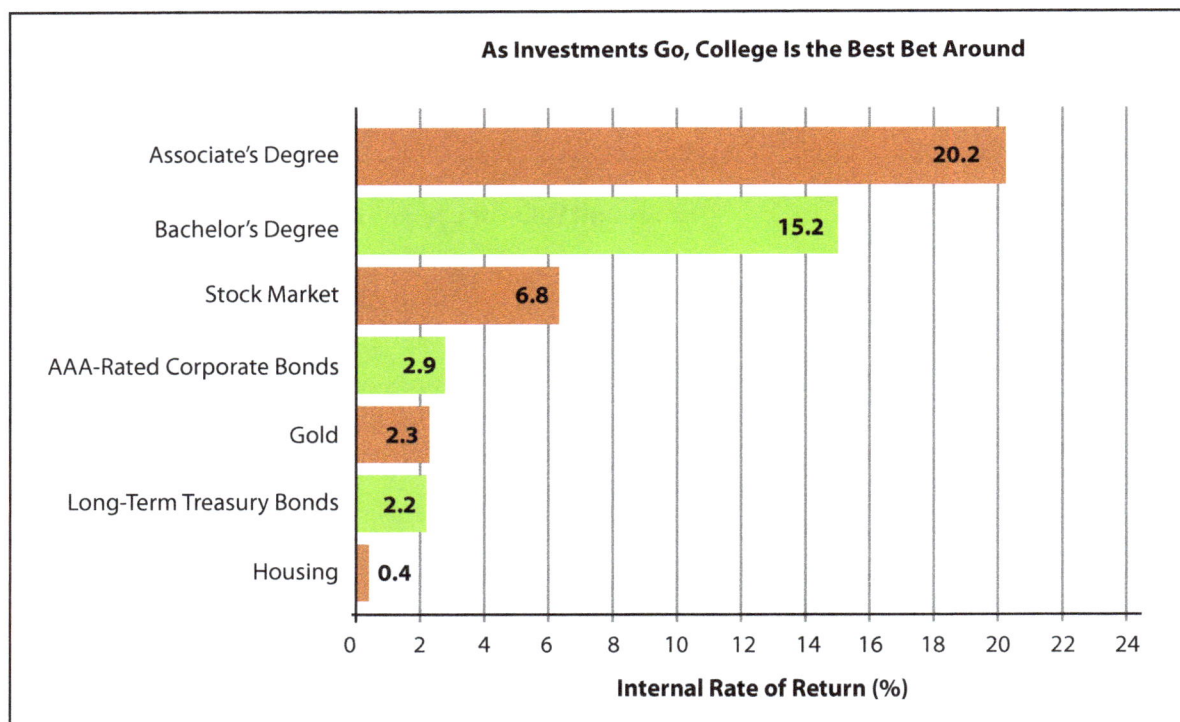

As Investments Go, College Is the Best Bet Around

Investment	Internal Rate of Return (%)
Associate's Degree	20.2
Bachelor's Degree	15.2
Stock Market	6.8
AAA-Rated Corporate Bonds	2.9
Gold	2.3
Long-Term Treasury Bonds	2.2
Housing	0.4

Figure 5   Rates of Return Compared.
Source: Adapted from The Hamilton Project 2012.

Employment Conditions and Job Security

Completion of at least some education after high school not only opens doors to hundreds of more jobs, but also better working conditions compared to just graduating from high school alone. (Education Pays 2013: The Benefits of Higher Education for Individuals and Society, College Board). Furthermore, the likelihood of your child's continuous employment throughout his life increases with each level of college completed. Note these important findings confirmed by the Pathways to Prosperity study:

- College graduates find new jobs more easily than non-graduates.
- College graduates are far less likely to be unemployed than non-graduates.
- In 2010, 82 percent of adults with a bachelor's degree or higher were employed full-time as compared to only 67 percent with only a high school diploma.

- Adults who have earned at least an associate degree are significantly more likely to be employed than those who only have a high school diploma or less.

- As technology advances, more jobs will require some level of education or training, even for entry-level positions.

OTHER BENEFITS OF OBTAINING FURTHER EDUCATION AFTER HIGH SCHOOL

Financial income and stable employment are often emphasized as the primary benefits of obtaining a higher education, yet there are several other important outcomes and benefits to consider.

Increased Knowledge and Skills

A college education can help your child increase his knowledge in specific fields that may be available to him in the future. In addition, your child will be able to express himself better, think critically, and have a better understanding of the world around him.

Networking Opportunities

College students often meet others who have similar goals, yet different experiences and backgrounds. Your child will most likely develop a large network of friends in college. These friends will help him build a network of people whom he will be able to use as contacts to find career opportunities in his future. Not only will contacts made in college help find career opportunities, but also support other areas of his life.

Exposure to New Ideas and Experiences

New ideas and experiences enrich the lives of college students. College provides opportunities to meet and work with groups of people and communities who are diverse and whose experiences may be much different.

Personal Fulfillment

College will provide your child with tremendous opportunities for personal growth. Your child will be able to explore new subjects, meet many different types of people, and participate in activities he might not otherwise experience. A stimulating college environment can enrich your child for a lifetime.

Health and Lifestyle Benefits

Research shows that adults with a college education are more likely to live healthier lifestyles than their less-educated peers. Not only do college-educated adults earn more income and have better access to health care, they also smoke less, exercise more, and have lower obesity rates. These differences not only affect the lifestyles and life expectancies of these individuals, but also reduce medical costs for our society as a whole.

Additional facts regarding the health and lifestyle benefits of a college education are outlined in the Education Pays 2013 report from the College Board:

- Education plays a large role in understanding the dangers of tobacco use. The gap between the smoking rates of four-year college graduates and high school graduates was only 2 percentage points in 1962, yet with education, the gap jumped to 17 percentage points in 2012.

- Within all age groups, college-educated adults are less likely than others to be obese. In addition, children living in households with more educated parents are less likely than other children to be obese.

- Among young adults between the ages of 25 and 34, 68 percent of four-year college graduates exercised once a week as compared to only 40 percent of high school graduates.

- Those with higher levels of educational attainment are more likely than others to be covered by employer-provided health insurance.

- Adults with higher levels of education are more likely to engage in their communities, participate in volunteer work, understand political issues, and to vote.

- College-educated workers are more likely than others to be offered pension plans by their employers.

- Among workers ages 30 to 45 with a bachelor's degree or higher, 56 percent strongly agree that their jobs require them to keep learning new things. Among those with some college or an associate degree, 44 percent strongly agree with this statement, but only 30 percent of those with a high school diploma.

In summary, any education after high school—whether it is a certificate earned at a local community college or a doctorate degree—has tremendous benefits for your child. These benefits include:

- Financial security

- A lifetime of increased earning potential

- Increased lifetime employment opportunities

- Much lower chance of unemployment

- Positive employment conditions and job security

- Increased knowledge and skills in a variety of areas

- Networking opportunities

- Exposure to new ideas and experiences

- Personal fulfillment, increased overall health, and longer life expectancy

The remainder of this book is dedicated to giving you detailed information and resources to help you guide your child down the appropriate educational path, from the early years of elementary school through the completion of his college education.

Chapter 2

College Preparation Begins in Elementary School

"At the end of the day, the most overwhelming key to a child's success is the positive involvement of parents."
—Jane D. Hull, former U.S. Speaker of the House, 2015

In today's world, preparation for educational success must start at a very young age. Your child's college and career path choices will greatly depend upon how much she learns in elementary, middle, and high school. It is hard to believe that college preparation must start at such a young age, but research has shown that if children are lagging academically in the third grade, they generally stay behind throughout high school, lowering their chances of completing a college education (Strivetogether.org).

But there is good news. Our California educational system provides exceptional resources for both parents and students. These resources are there to assist children at all academic levels and to help ensure that each student can have a bright academic future. In this chapter, we will cover the most important tips, resources, and strategies to help your child succeed—both academically and socially—in elementary school.

CHOOSING THE RIGHT ELEMENTARY SCHOOL FOR YOUR CHILD

Pre-Kindergarten and Kindergarten—Ages Four to Six

Several elementary school districts in California now use a "Kindergarten Readiness Assessment" tool to help determine if your child is ready to enter and be successful in kindergarten. As a parent, you can play a large part in your child's educational success by teaching and reinforcing the following skills she needs to be successful in her first formal year of education. Before starting kindergarten, your child should be able to:

- Hold a book correctly and retell stories

- Sort objects by color, shape, and size

- Know his/her first and last name

- Be familiar with letters and numbers

- Show curiosity about new things

- Stay with a task until completed

- Follow basic rules and routines

- Get along with others

- Know how to share and take turns

- Follow two-step directions

- Verbally communicate needs and ideas

- Use sentences of at least five or six words

- Demonstrate self-help skills such as dressing, toileting, and eating

- Hold a pencil and cut with scissors

Source: First Five—CA Department of Health and Human Resources, 2015.

Parents have several options when choosing an elementary school. The choices can often be confusing and overwhelming to new parents, especially since most of us grew up with no other option except to attend the local neighborhood school. Currently in California, parents can choose between traditional public schools, public charter schools, private schools, and homeschool options.

- Traditional public schools are free and are usually managed by a school district. Local public schools draw students from a defined geographic area called an "attendance zone." Most children go to a public school located in their attendance zone. However, many school districts throughout the state offer "open enrollment" or "interdistrict transfer agreements." Open enrollment provides students enrolled in one of over 1,000 Open Enrollment California schools the option to enroll in a school within the same district, or any other district, provided the school to which they are applying has a higher Academic Performance Index (API) score than the student's school of residence. In addition, interdistrict transfer agreements allow families to request that their child attend a school outside of the attendance zone /district where they live. If you are thinking about requesting a transfer, check with both the school in your district and the school where you'd like to send your child. Both schools and/or districts involved must agree to the transfer request.

- Public charter schools are a unique alternative to traditional public schools. These schools operate under a "charter" that gives them permission from a local or state educational agency to operate. The charter outlines certain standards for student performance that must be met. However, these schools do not have the same rules and regulations as traditional public schools. Public charter schools are free and many have a particular area of focus such as nature, science, or the arts.

- Private schools do not receive public tax dollars to operate and are run by private organizations. Parents must pay tuition to send their children to a private school. Other private funds may support the private school's operation.

- Homeschooling is another alternative schooling choice for families. Homeschooling is highly personalized, yet it follows state- and district-approved courses of study for each grade level. Parents choosing to homeschool must work closely with a credentialed teacher(s) or program to meet minimal educational requirements.

TIPS FOR CHOOSING THE RIGHT ELEMENTARY SCHOOL FOR YOUR CHILD

Now that your child is ready and excited to start kindergarten, what are your next steps as a parent to ensure her success? Below are some tips and strategies for you as a parent and which will help lead to your child's success, even before her first day of school.

You should first visit the different types of schools you are considering. Most elementary schools offer tours and will let you visit a kindergarten classroom. In some cases you may be able to meet the kindergarten teachers. Some schools offer a "Kindergarten Orientation," which is a special day where families can visit the campus, meet teachers and staff, and learn about the school.

- Take into account what you know about your child's personality, temperament, etc.

- Think about how your child might do in the classroom environment you observe.

- Consider whether the school has the services and activities you will need (after-school care, tutoring, help learning English, etc.).

- Talk with teachers, principals, and (if possible) parents of students already enrolled.

- Research possible schools online.

RESEARCHING POTENTIAL SCHOOLS ONLINE

Researching the academic performance of schools has become relatively easy for parents. The California Department of Education has an enormous amount of information specifically for parents located at http://www.cde.ca.gov/re/di/po/parents.asp.

On this site, the following information can be found for each elementary school you may be considering for your child:

School Accountability Report Card (SARC)

Since 1988, state law has required all public schools receiving state funding to prepare and distribute a SARC. The SARC is a type of report card that provides parents and the community with important information about each public school. A SARC can be an effective way for a school to report on its progress in achieving goals. The public may also use a SARC to evaluate and compare schools on a variety of indicators.

What information does the SARC contain?   Although there is great variation in the design of these school report cards, they generally begin with a profile that provides background information about the school and its students. The profile usually summarizes the school's mission, goals, and accomplishments. Additionally, state law requires that the SARC contain all of the following:

- Demographic data: Number, ethnicity, and ages of students

- Information on school safety and climate for learning

- Academic data

- School year completion rates

- Class sizes

- Teacher and staff information

- Curriculum and instruction descriptions

- Higher education preparation information

- Fiscal and expenditure data

After conducting your online research, finalize your decision by narrowing your choices down to at least three schools and then do the following in order to make your final decision:

- Meet with the school administrators and ask for a tour of the school.

- Visit a classroom and ask if you can sit in briefly.

- Obtain a copy of the school's site plan.

- Communicate with potential teachers (via phone or e-mail) to get a sense of their teaching styles.

YOU FOUND A GREAT ELEMENTARY SCHOOL! NOW WHAT?

Understanding the Language of Elementary Schools

As an elementary school parent, the language or terminology used by the educators at your child's new school can sometimes be intimidating and confusing. Elementary school principals, teachers, and counselors often speak in abbreviated terms or acronyms to quickly communicate with their fellow educators at school. Often, these acronyms can be very confusing to parents. Following are some of the most common terms that will be used at the elementary school level, with explanations for each term.

SSC (School Site Council)   The SSC consists of a group of teachers, parents, students, administrators, and interested community members who meet generally once a month to develop and monitor a school's improvement plan.

PTA (Parent-Teacher Association)   The PTA is an association consisting of parents and teachers who assist with raising money for school programs and serve as a liaison between parents and school administrators.

GATE (Gifted And Talented Education)   The GATE Program offers educational opportunities for students in state public elementary and secondary schools who have been identified as gifted and talented based on their high academic performance and who demonstrate the capability of achieving significantly beyond the level of their peers.

IEP (Individualized Education Program)   The IEP is a document that helps identify and meet the educational needs of children with emotional, learning, or physical disabilities.

Federal law requires that all children with disabilities receive a free and appropriate education according to the development of an annual Individualized Education Program (IEP).

SARC (School Accountability Report Card)   As mentioned earlier, the SARC is a report that schools update annually to inform parents and the community on the achievement, environment, resources, and demographics of their student population.

ELL (English Language Learners)   Students who speak a language other than English at home and are learning English as a second language are referred to as English Language Learners.

TITLE I   This is a federally- and state-funded program for low-income and disadvantaged students. These funds are awarded to schools to address the unique educational needs of low-income students who are academically below grade level.

ELAC (English Learner Advisory Committee)   This is an advisory group made up of parents and other community members that makes recommendations to the school regarding programs for students who are ELL students. ELACs provide parents of ELL students with opportunities to:

- Learn more about the programs being offered to their children.
- Participate in the school's needs assessment of students, parents, and teachers.
- Provide input on the most effective ways to support full participation of ELL students in all school activities.
- Provide input on the most effective ways to ensure regular school attendance.

DELAC (District-Level English Learner Advisory Committee)   The DELAC committee consists of representatives of a district's ELACs and who advise the district on programs and services for English learners.

CUMULATIVE FILE   The student cumulative file provides a continuous and current record about a student's academic performance and growth. Cumulative record data are collected to provide school personnel with information to assist students academically.

AERIES (Aeries Student Information System)   The Aeries SIS is an online student data management system for K–12 schools which supports the requirements established by the California Department of Education as well as other state and federal reporting mandates. Parents can access grades, test scores, and other student information by visiting the Aeries link provided on a school's website.

SCHOOL TESTING AND ASSESSMENT TERMS

Signed into law on October 2, 2013, California Assembly Bill 484 launched a new student testing system for California's schools, now called the California Assessment of Student Performance and Progress (CAASPP). The CAASPP system is based on the new California Common Core State Standards for English–language arts and mathematics. This new system replaced the Standardized Testing and Reporting (STAR) Program that was based on 1997 standards.

The primary goal of the new statewide testing program is to better prepare all students for college and careers in the twenty-first century. Computer-based assessments, developed through the Smarter Balanced Assessment Consortium, form the cornerstone for CAASPP.

Common Core State Standards (CCSS)

Common Core standards are referred to as "academic norms" that define what students should learn at each grade level. Although there are academic standards for each content area, the four core areas are English Language Arts, Mathematics, History-Social Science, and Science.

The CCS Standards are a logical progression of learning goals in English language arts and mathematics from K–12 grades. The CCSS outlines what is expected academically of all students at each grade level, thereby ensuring that students, parents, teachers, and school administrators are working toward the same academic goals. While most states already have English language arts and mathematics standards in place, the standards often vary widely from state to state. Having the same standards in place nationally helps all students obtain a good education, even if they change schools or move to a different state.

Teachers, parents, and education experts developed these standards to prepare ALL students for success in college and the workplace.

Smarter Balanced Assessment Consortium (SBAC)

The former California Standards Tests (CST) were recently replaced by the Smarter Balanced Assessment Consortium tests. The SBAC assessments are computer-based, are aligned to the Common Core Standards previously mentioned, and are very different than older tests involving paper and pencil. Also, the new SBAC assessment asks more than multiple-choice questions. Students have to prepare short essay answers for some questions and even work with other students to tackle multipart assignments. This allows students to complete an in-depth project that demonstrates classroom skills and real-world problem solving. One of the advantages to this new assessment is that schools and parents will receive computerized SBAC results in weeks, instead of months. Quicker results mean that schools and teachers can use the information to develop their instruction to better meet the unique academic needs of their students. In addition, teachers will be able to use the results to identify exactly what each student needs to focus on so that he/she can continue to improve academically. The SBAC is also being used to provide possible exemptions for 11th grade students for the California State University Placement Tests.

STS (Standards-Based Tests in Spanish)

The STS are multiple-choice tests required for Spanish-speaking EL students in grades 2 through 11 who have either been enrolled in school for less than twelve cumulative (not consecutive) months on the first day of regular school testing or are receiving instruction in Spanish regardless of the length of time they have been enrolled in school. These tests assess reading-language arts and mathematics in Spanish.

CMA (California Modified Assessment)

The CMA is a grade-level assessment for students in grades 3 through 11 who have an IEP, are receiving grade-level instruction, and will not achieve grade-level proficiency within the year even with intervention. The purpose of these tests is to allow students with disabilities to demonstrate achievement of the content standards in English-language arts, writing, mathematics, and science.

"My teacher sends report cards as PDF attachments. Luckily, my parents have no idea how to open computer files."

PARENTING STRATEGIES AND TIPS FOR ELEMENTARY SCHOOL SUCCESS

Every parent wants his or her child to succeed in elementary school, starting on the first day. Some parents seem to instinctively know what to do to help their child succeed, while for the rest of us, the learning curve can be steep. Following are just a few strategies that will help you as a parent of a new elementary school student during the first few months of the school year.

Reach out to Your Child's Teachers

Start by attending the "Meet-the-Teacher" night, parent orientation, Back-to-School night, or other similar events at the beginning of every school year. But don't stop there. Make a point of introducing yourself to your child's teachers and learning about classroom activities and their expectations for the new year. Also, find out how each teacher prefers to communicate. Many use e-mail as their main form of contact, but phone calls and individual meetings are usually welcome as well. Today, many teachers even use text messaging for your convenience.

Set a Routine

Establish healthy home routines for school days, such as a consistent bedtime, wake-up time, and getting ready for school patterns. Decide on a regular homework time and create a comfortable and quiet workspace in the home. Set bedtimes that allow your child to get at least ten to twelve hours of sleep each night.

Stay Organized

Help your child stay on top of school, activity, and team sport schedules with a calendar posted in your home or online.

Plan Ahead for an Easy, Healthy Breakfast

Children who eat a healthy breakfast each morning have more energy available for learning. Try simple and protein-loaded breakfast options like breakfast burritos, bagels with cream cheese, waffles with peanut butter, or yogurt and fruit smoothies.

Become a Class Parent or Class Volunteer

Consider becoming a class parent to develop a closer relationship with teachers and get an inside look into what goes on in the classroom without having to commit to a lot of time. Class parents organize other parent volunteers for parties and events, help create newsletters, or perhaps document the school year in photos. Class volunteers help the teacher or students in a variety of ways, easily staying abreast of their child's success and teacher's expectations.

Encourage a Strong Foundation in Reading and Math

Strong academic competency in math and reading is critical for every child. When students begin to struggle in reading and math in the early grades of K–5, it can make academic success much harder to achieve in later grades. If academic performance in reading or math is a problem, parents need to address it immediately before their child loses interest in school and other subjects. The following tips will help you work with teachers to develop an academic plan that will help increase your child's performance and allow her to complete academic work at grade level.

LITERATURE

"JUST THINK OF IT AS IF YOU'RE READING
A LONG TEXT-MESSAGE."

STRATEGIES TO PROMOTE A STRONG FOUNDATION IN READING AND MATH

Communicate with Your Child's Teacher

Many schools schedule parent-teacher conferences in the months of October and November. Attending these meetings should be a priority for all parents. This is your chance to see how things are going academically and emotionally with your child and to communicate with her teachers on how to improve her performance. Ask questions such as: "What can we be doing at home to practice what my child is learning?" The National Parent Teacher Association has created grade-level Parents' Guides to Student Success that can be a great resource for what to discuss at these conferences. Visit www.pta.org/parentsguide for more information.

At parent-teacher conferences, you want to:

- Be prepared to listen, talk, and take notes.

- Write out your questions before you meet with the teacher.

- Ask for specific information about your child's work and progress.

- Review what the teacher has told you and follow up by talking with your child.

- Check back with the teacher regularly to see how things are going as the year progresses.

Seek Extra Help

Does it seem your child is having trouble keeping up with a specific subject area? Ask the teacher about school-sponsored tutoring programs and resources to help reinforce her learning outside of class. Many teachers also offer extra help during office hours before or after school.

Consistently Review All Report Cards or Online Portals

Make sure to pay careful attention to all report cards and/or grades, particularly the first report that comes out in early fall. You want to get help for any behavior or academic problem areas that may be revealed in these reports before your child falls too far behind. Ask your child's teacher how grades are determined and for suggestions on how your child can improve, if needed. Review grades and the teacher's comments with your child—always starting with something she is doing well before pointing out areas that need attention, and then ending with something positive again.

Read and Then Read Some More

Take time at home to read aloud each day with your child and take turns reading. Encourage older children to read on their own and to their younger siblings. Anything that interests them—from comic books to the classics—counts. Read to your children until they can read to you or to themselves. A child who enjoys reading will enjoy school more than one who doesn't like to read. Visit your local library and ask the librarian to suggest books if you aren't sure what your child will like or if you have a limited number of books at home.

Get Art and Music Smart

Exposure to art and music can help your child excel in math, problem solving, reading, and will help her develop teamwork skills and self-esteem. Check out the resources on www. free.ed.gov and stock up on arts and crafts supplies. Let your child experiment with inexpensive music-makers like a harmonica, a recorder, or an old guitar. Check out music CDs and art books from your library and urge older siblings to join their school's choir, band, or drama programs.

Get "Schooled" in Math

Ask your child's teachers for suggestions on math games and online activities you can do with her at home. For additional resources, visit the National Council of Teachers of Mathematics at http://www.nctm.org/

Encourage and Expect Consistent School Attendance

Students can only learn if they attend school. Students who regularly miss school fall behind other students, regardless of their intelligence. Their classmates may also stop asking them to participate in class activities and other social or sporting events. Missing too many days of school may also cause students to lose interest in school and to drop out.

STRATEGIES TO PROMOTE CONSISTENT SCHOOL ATTENDANCE

Ask about School

Find the time to speak with your child on a daily basis, especially about topics that she is interested in. Ask about both the good and the bad in school and keep an ear open for experiences your child may not want to talk about.

Use College Words at Home

Let your child know that there is an exciting reason why she is attending school every day. That reason is college! Regularly use college-related vocabulary words and terms in your daily conversations with your child to get her excited about her future. The following table offers some grade-level words that may help promote college awareness for your child. Note that these terms will be explained in detail in later chapters.

Kindergarten	College, Education
Grade 1	Achieve, Career, Graduate, Goal
Grade 2	Major, Mascot, Professor, Dorm, Scholarship
Grade 3	Advisor, Application, Dean's List, GPA, Bachelor's Degree
Grades 4 and 5	All words K–3 and College entrance course requirements—"A–G"

Table 3   College Awareness Terms to Use in Elementary School

Communicate with the Teacher

Meet with your child's teacher to discuss her academic progress. Let the teacher or teachers know when important changes are happening in your family's life, such as the death of a relative, a move to a new home, or anything that might affect your child's behavior, attendance, or performance at school—so that school staff can offer their support and/ or accommodations as well.

Acknowledge Your Child's Potential Test Anxiety

Many students experience test anxiety and may not want to go to school on state testing days. Make a note of the state testing schedule on your family calendar so you can reassure your child that these tests will not be graded and that they will be used to measure her learning for that school year. Be sure that your child gets a good night's rest and eats a healthy breakfast on the morning of all testing days.

Realize That Healthy Self-Confidence Is Just as Important as Academics

Positive self-confidence and self-esteem are extremely important to the success of your child in elementary school. Negative social and/or emotional experiences—in the home, the classroom, or on the playground—could affect your child's academic performance and attendance. If left unchecked, these negative experiences could greatly impact your child's academic performance in school.

STRATEGIES TO PROMOTE SELF-CONFIDENCE IN YOUR CHILD

- Motivate your child to assume more responsibilities around the house and develop new abilities and skills. This will increase her confidence in new abilities.
- Frequently demonstrate how much you love your child, regardless of whether or not you approve of her behavior.
- Maintain positive communication by remembering to always focus on finding solutions to problems and having your child give you her ideas of solutions to problems.
- Participate in all events in which your child is involved in to show her how important she is to you.
- Encourage your child to participate in activities in addition to her regular school work. Some examples include: practicing a sport, playing an instrument in the school band,

doing volunteer work, and/or taking on a leadership role at school. There are many benefits for participating in extracurricular activities, such as making new friends, discovering new abilities, learning to work as part of a team, and developing self-confidence.

- Ask about your child's school friends and invite them over for play dates. Get to know the parents of her friends to gain a better understanding of each schoolmate's home life.

- Teach your child to set goals and finish her projects. This will help her develop a sense of accomplishment and satisfaction.

LEARN ABOUT THE HARMFUL EFFECTS OF BULLYING

Most children have been teased by a sibling or a friend at some point. It's not usually harmful when done in a playful, friendly, and mutual way, and both children find it funny. However, when teasing becomes hurtful, unkind, and constant, it crosses the line into bullying and needs to stop.

The U.S. Department of Health and Human Services (HHS) defines bullying as unwanted, aggressive behavior among school-aged children that involves a real or perceived power imbalance. The behavior is repeated, or has the potential to be repeated, over time. Both kids who are bullied and who bully others may have serious, lasting problems.

Bullying is defined as student behavior that is aggressive and includes:

- **An imbalance of power:** Kids who bully use their power—such as physical strength, access to embarrassing information, or popularity—to control or harm others. Power imbalances can change over time and in different situations, even if they involve the same people.

- **Repetition:** Bullying behaviors happen more than once or have the potential to happen more than once.

  Bullying includes actions such as making threats, spreading rumors, attacking someone physically or verbally, and excluding someone from a group on purpose.

There are three types of bullying (Source: U.S. Department of Health and Human Services):

Verbal bullying is saying or writing mean things. Verbal bullying includes:

- Teasing
- Name-calling

- Inappropriate sexual comments
- Taunting
- Threatening to cause harm

Social bullying, sometimes referred to as "relational bullying," involves hurting someone's reputation or relationships. Social bullying includes:

- Excluding someone on purpose
- Telling other children not to be friends with someone
- Spreading rumors about someone
- Embarrassing someone in public

Physical bullying involves hurting a person's body or possessions. Physical bullying includes:

- Hitting/kicking/pinching
- Spitting
- Tripping/pushing
- Taking or breaking someone's things
- Making mean or rude hand gestures

Why Children Bully

Why Kids Bully

Kids bully for a variety of reasons. Sometimes bullying behavior stems from children who have uncontrolled anger. They pick on kids because they need a victim—someone who seems emotionally or physically weaker, or just acts or appears different in some way—to feel more important, popular, or in control. Although some bullies are bigger or stronger than their victims, that's not always the case.

Sometimes kids torment others because that's the way they've been treated, or because there are not consequences for their actions at home. They may think their behavior is normal because they come from families or other settings where everyone regularly gets angry, shouts, or calls names. Some popular TV shows and video games highlight violence, and some even seem to promote meanness—people are "voted off," shunned, or ridiculed for their appearance or lack of talent.

Note the Following Common Situations Faced by Students:

Situation #1—Every day 10-year-old Seth asked his mom for more and more lunch money. Yet he seemed to be getting thinner and was always hungry when he came home from school. It turned out that Seth was giving his lunch money over to a fifth-grader who was threatening to beat him up if he did not give up the money.

Situation #2—Kayla, 13, thought things were going well at her new school since all the popular girls were being so nice to her. But then she found out that one of them had posted mean rumors about her on the Internet. Kayla started going to the nurse's office complaining of a stomachache to avoid the girls in study hall and would cry herself to sleep at night.

Unfortunately, the kind of bullying that Seth and Kayla experienced above is very common and widespread.

WHAT DO YOU DO IF YOU SUSPECT YOUR CHILD IS BEING "BULLIED"?

Signs That Your Child May Be Being Bullied

Unless your child tells you about bullying—or has visible bruises or injuries—it can be difficult to figure out if it is occurring. Look for the following warning signs: Your child is acting differently or seeming anxious; she is not eating or sleeping well; or she is not doing the things she usually enjoys. When kids seem moodier or more easily upset than usual, or when they start avoiding certain situations, like taking the bus to school, it might be because of a bully.

If you suspect bullying but your child is reluctant to open up, then seek opportunities to bring up the issue. For instance, you might see a situation on a TV show and use it as a conversation starter asking "What do you think of this?" or "What do you think that person should have done?" This might lead to questions like: "Have you ever seen this happen?" or "Have you ever experienced this?" You might want to talk about any experiences you or another family member had at that same age. Let your child know that if she is being bullied—or sees it happening to someone else—that it is so important for her to talk to someone about it—you, a teacher, a school counselor, a family friend, or sibling.

Helping Children Deal with Bullying

If your child tells you about someone bullying her, focus on offering comfort and support—no matter how upset you are. Kids are often reluctant to tell adults about bullying because they feel embarrassed and ashamed that it is happening or worry that their parents will be disappointed in them. Sometimes kids feel like it is their own fault and that if they only looked or acted differently then it would not be happening. Sometimes they are scared that if the bully finds out that they told on him/her, then it will only get worse. Others are worried that their parents will not believe them or do anything about it. Other kids worry that their parents will urge them to fight back when they are really scared to fight. Instead, praise your child for being brave enough to talk about it. Remind your child that she is not alone—a lot of people get bullied at some point. Emphasize that it is the bully who is behaving badly—not your child. Reassure your child that you will figure out what to do about it together.

Tell the School   Most schools want to be notified if you suspect a bullying situation with your child. Many schools have bullying rules and policies. Find out about what these policies are at your child's school. In certain cases, you may need to contact legal authorities if you have serious concerns about your child's safety and the school is not responsive.

Get Help   Sometimes an older sibling, cousin, or friend can help deal with the situation. It may help your daughter to hear how the older sister she idolizes was teased about her braces, for example, and how she dealt with it. An older sibling or friend also might be able to give you some perspective on what is happening at school or wherever the bullying is happening, and help you figure out the best solution. Take it seriously if you hear that the bullying will get worse if the bully finds out that your child reported him or her. Teachers or counselors are the best people to contact first.

Reaching out for Help   At home you can lessen the impact of the bullying by encouraging your child to get together with friends who help build her confidence. Help your child meet other kids by joining clubs or sports programs and find activities that can help her feel confident and strong, such as a self-defense class. Remember, as upsetting as bullying can be for you and your family, lots of people and resources are available to help.

PARENT KNOWLEDGE AND ACTION ARE KEY TO ELEMENTARY SCHOOL SUCCESS

By using and building upon the information and strategies outlined in this chapter, you can help to ensure that your child will have a positive and successful experience in elementary school. Before you know it, your child will graduate from these early years of elementary education and move on to the next critical stage in her preparation for college—middle school!

Chapter 3

The Middle School Years

"I've never run into a person who yearns for their middle school days"
—Jeff Kinney, Author of "Diary of a Wimpy Kid"

Your child will face many changes when he transitions from elementary to middle school. These changes include having several teachers throughout the day instead of just one, adapting to different teaching styles, and understanding new grading systems. It is during the middle school years that your child will build a strong foundation for his academic preparation and self-esteem, both incredibly necessary to prepare him for his high school experience ahead. During the middle school years, your child will also begin to search for his own sense of identity and independence from you, which makes his friends and fellow students a stronger and more direct influence in his life. Even so, it is important to remember that this stage in your child's life still requires special attention from you. Research has determined that preteens do much better academically and socially in school when their parents are directly involved in their lives (National Middle School Association 2014).

Although helping your child achieve academic success in middle school will require a lot of time, dedication, and careful planning, it will be well worth the effort! The better prepared your child is academically in middle school, the more academic options he will have in high school and eventually in college. Your child's academic preparation will also provide him with the skills and knowledge necessary throughout life to succeed in his chosen career.

The following are important tasks and strategies you can do as a parent to help your child succeed in middle school:

SIX IMPORTANT PARENT TIPS BEFORE THE MIDDLE SCHOOL YEAR BEGINS

Tip #1.   Talk, talk, talk!

Try to have a conversation with your child about his fears and excitement about going to middle school, even though he may find it difficult to talk about it. Discuss any concerns your child may have before starting the school year. Your child may have concerns about having several teachers, getting to class on time, finding the cafeteria and/or locker, navigating crowded hallways, and/or having more homework. Assure him that middle school is a time of emotional, physical, and academic transition for everyone—including all of his friends and fellow students.

Tip #2.   Learn about your child's developmental changes

This is a time of changes for how teenagers think, feel, and interact with others, and how their bodies grow. Most girls will be physically mature by now, and most will have completed puberty. Boys might still be maturing physically during this time. Your child might have concerns about his body size, shape, or weight. Eating disorders also can be common, especially among girls. During this time, your pre-teen is developing his unique personality and opinions. Relationships with friends are still important, yet he will have other interests as he develops a more clear sense of who he is. This is also an important time to prepare for more independence and responsibility; many teenagers start working, and many will be leaving home soon after high school.

Emotional/Social Changes

Children in this age group might:

- Have more interest in the opposite sex
- Go through more or less conflict with parents
- Show more independence from parents
- Have a deeper capacity for caring and sharing and for developing more intimate relationships

- Spend less time with parents and more time with friends
- Feel a lot of sadness or depression, which can lead to poor grades at school, alcohol or drug use, unsafe sex, and other problems

Thinking and Learning Changes

Children in this age group might:

- Learn more defined work habits
- Show more concern about future school and work plans
- Be better able to give reasons for their own choices, including about what is right or wrong

Tip #3.   Discover your child's dominant learning style

All human beings possess different types of intelligence and learning styles. Your child most likely has a specific learning style that is more dominant than others due to genetic makeup, background, and age. Assessment tools, such as the VARK Learning Style Assessment, will help determine your child's current learning style and/or strengths. This tool can be found at http://www.vark-learn.com.

The VARK Assessment Identifies Four Learning Styles

Visual (V)

A visual learner prefers to learn from information in maps, diagrams, charts, graphs, flow charts, circles, and other devices people use to represent what could be represented in words. For example, when a whiteboard is used to draw a visual diagram for the subject being taught—that will be most helpful for those students with a visual preference.

Auditory (A)

An auditory learner prefers information that is "heard or spoken." Auditory learners report they learn best from lectures, group discussion, radio, e-mail, using mobile phones, speaking, web-chat, and talking things through. E-mail is included here because, although it is text and could be included in the reading/writing category (below), it is often written in chat style with abbreviations, slang, and non-formal language. Auditory preference includes speaking out loud as well as to oneself. Often, people with this preference want to sort things out by speaking first, rather than sorting out their ideas and then speaking. They may say again what has already been said, or ask an obvious and previously answered question. They have a need to say it themselves in order to learn.

Reading/Writing (R)

This learning preference is for information relayed by using words. Not surprisingly, many teachers and students have a strong preference for this learning mode. This preference emphasizes text-based reading and writing in all forms, but especially manuals, reports, essays, and assignments. People who prefer this learning style are often attracted to the Internet, lists, diaries, dictionaries, quotations, and words, words, words.

Kinesthetic (K)

By definition, this learning style refers to people who prefer to be connected to reality, "either through concrete personal experiences, examples, practice or simulation." People with this learning style enjoy demonstrations, simulations, videos, and movies of "real" things, as well as case studies, practice, and applications. The key to this style is the concrete nature of the example. If it can be grasped, held, tasted, or felt it will probably be well received. People with this as a strong preference learn from the experience of doing something and they value their own background experiences and, less so, experiences of others.

What about Mixtures of Learning Styles? (MM)

There are seldom instances where only one learning style is used, or is sufficient, so that is why there is a four-part VARK profile. The VARK questionnaire provides four scores and also includes a mixture of the four learning modes. Those students who do not have a standout mode with one strong preference well above other scores are defined as multimodal, or MM, learners.

Discovering your child's dominant learning style will help you identify his strengths and weaknesses in order to share this information with his teachers and counselors.

Tip #4.   Communicate with middle school staff

As a parent of a new middle school student, you should visit the school and introduce yourself to staff before the school year begins. Questions you should ask the principal and/or teachers include:

- Is there a transition/orientation program for students leaving elementary school and entering middle school?
- Is there a middle school tour available to both parents and students?

- How are students tested and placed in math courses?

- What electives are offered to students?

- Are school counselors available in the summer before school begins to help select course schedules?

- Can parents volunteer at the school?

- What extracurricular activities, music, art, and/or sporting activities are available in this middle school?

- Does the school have a daily electronic bulletin board with which to communicate with parents?

- Does the school offer an anti-drugs/anti-drinking prevention program?

- Does the school have a bullying prevention program?

Tip #5.   Meet with the school counselor

It is never too early to ensure that your child is taking the right classes that will prepare him for high school graduation and college admission. Meet with your child's counselor and ask him about the courses your child will be taking each semester. It is extremely important that you inform your child's counselor that your expectation is for your child to go to college.

What Does a School Counselor DO?

- Assists students with the selection of their classes each semester.

- Maintains a record of the classes each student is enrolled in and the grades earned.

- Informs students and their parents about academic progress in all subjects, especially in core subjects such as English and math.

- Refers students to additional academic and support services available at the school.

- Provides students with information on how to prepare for college.

Questions Parents Should Ask the School Counselor

- How did my child score on his most recent standardized test?

- Are there any academic support programs available? How can he participate in any pre-college programs?

- Are my child's classes considered college preparation courses?

- Is my child enrolled in the appropriate math classes that will prepare him to take high school math classes?

- What electives do you recommend for college-bound students?

- What activities should my child do at home or during the summer to ensure success in middle school?

- Is my child meeting academic standards for each course or subject?

- What classes should my child take if his current course placement seems too easy? How does my child compare academically to his grade-level peers?

- What can I do to ensure that my child will be at the appropriate academic level required for high school courses and eventually college admissions?

Tip #6. Become familiar with the terms "Core Courses" and "A-G" requirements

Core Courses

California requires all students to meet academic content standards that correspond to their grade level. Every middle school student in California must complete the following four core subjects during each semester of his middle school years:

- History/Social Studies
- English/Language Arts
- Mathematics
- Science

"A-G" Course Requirements

The "A-G" course requirements are the high school courses required for admission to both California State University (CSU) and University of California (UC) systems. The intent of "A-G" requirements is to ensure that students attain a level of knowledge that will prepare them for more advanced study when they begin college.

Even though A-G high school course requirements generally do not begin until high school, middle school is the best time for your child to prepare to succeed in these important courses for college admission. As an active parent, you should request a copy of your child's class schedule and review it to ensure that he is enrolled or will be enrolled in appropriate courses that will prepare him to take and complete high school "A-G" courses required for college admission. Most of the time, this means correct placement in a middle school math class that will prepare your child to meet or exceed the math requirement series of courses required for college admission.

TEN STRATEGIES TO HELP YOUR CHILD <u>DURING</u> THE MIDDLE SCHOOL YEARS

1. Encourage organization and self-discipline

During middle school, your child must learn to improve his organizational skills, take better notes, and study more effectively. These skills will help him be successful in high school and later in college. You can help your child strengthen his organization and self-discipline skills in the following ways:

- Provide your child with a quiet and well-lit place to do homework.

- Monitor your child's computer use, as school homework often requires your child to use a computer.

- Turn off the TV and cell phone until after all homework is completed.

- Develop a system that allows your child to organize important documents such as color-coded folders to file homework assignments per subject, or binders with dividers to separate material from each class.

- Make sure your child has a planner to record due dates for each homework assignment.

"So, for every day that your math grade stays below a B, your father will post a video of himself on YouTube."

- Motivate your child to develop a schedule or work plan that will help him manage time spent on each assignment.

- Show your child how to divide a large project into smaller projects to avoid feeling stressed or overwhelmed.

- Make an appointment with your child's teacher if you notice him struggling with a particular subject.

2. Monitor your child's grade point average

A good grade point average (GPA) is very important for students to maintain throughout their years in middle school. Students who have a high GPA (3.0 or higher) and have taken regular classes at their academic grade level should be able to take more rigorous courses, such as Advanced Placement (AP) and honors classes in high school. Parents should be aware that students who are better prepared and have a higher grade point average end up having a greater possibility of being admitted to a four-year university.

How to Calculate Your Child's Grade Point Average

Calculating your child's GPA is a relatively easy process. The letter grades from regular classes have the following point value:

A = 4 points   B = 3 points   C = 2 points   D = 1 point   F = 0 points

See the following table for a sample. Multiply the credit hours for each class times the grade points earned. For example, for a biology class worth three credit hours, three would be multiplied by four, since your child received an "A" in his biology class. The total grade points for that class would be 12.

Sample Student Transcript			
Course	**Credit Hours**	**Grade**	**Grade Points**
Biology	3	A (4 pts)	12
History	3	B (3 pts)	9
English	3	C (2 pts)	6
Mathematics	3	B (3 pts)	9
12 Total Credit Hours Attempted			36 Total Grade Points
Total Grade Points/ Total Credit Hours Attempted		36/12	= 3.00

Table 4   Calculating Grade Point Average

The final step is to divide the total grade points by the total credit hours attempted to calculate your child's G.P.A.

Additional Grade Points Can Be Earned in High School

Keep in mind that in advanced placement (AP) classes and some honors classes in high school, some schools award an additional point to each letter grade or additional points to a numeric score. This means that it is possible for students taking these high school classes to have a grade point average between a 4.0–5.0. Every school is different, so find out from your school counselor.

3. Ask detailed questions at all parent-teacher conferences

Some examples of questions you might want to ask at all parent-teacher conferences are:

- How can I track my child's academic progress?
- Is my child having any difficulties in your class? How can we help him at home?
- Have you noticed any learning issues/problems my child may have? If so, how can I request an evaluation and additional support?
- What is the best time and way (e-mail, phone, etc.) to contact you?
- How often do you give tests in your class?
- How is my child doing on the tests and quizzes in your class?
- Is my child below, at, or above academic level?
- How much time should my child spend on homework each day? What can I do to help him?
- Can you show me sample work that corresponds to my child's grade level to demonstrate how he should be performing?
- What are my child's grades? Does he need extra help? Does the school offer tutoring or other similar services? If so, when?

4. Emphasize the importance of reading

Reading is one of the most important skills your child should possess if he wants to succeed in college. Developing strong reading skills can also help your child succeed in other aspects of life. Reading is part of our daily adult activities in one way or another. We read when we check our mail, work, fill out an application or contract, find a street address, and follow instructions from a manual or a doctor's written prescription. The decisions we make about important matters can be greatly influenced by our ability to read. Individuals who read well have a broader vision of the world that surrounds them, allowing them to analyze information with a more critical perspective. Reading allows students to prepare themselves academically and professionally to obtain better jobs and become productive members of their communities.

Since reading is beneficial for everyone, you should ensure that your child develops and strengthens this skill. The sooner you incorporate reading as a habit, the more likely your child will maintain an interest in reading throughout his education and life.

Reading and Middle School Students   It would seem that the pre-teen years and reading do not always go hand-in-hand. During this developmental stage, your child is surrounded by many activities that will distract him from reading, such as spending time with friends, talking on the phone or texting, listening to music, watching TV, playing video games, or being online. These distractions pose a challenge as you look for ways to get him interested in reading.

How to Encourage Your Child to Read   A great way of motivating your child to read is by relating it to something that sparks his interest. For example, if he is interested in football, you can encourage him to find a book about his favorite team or football player. Afterward, you can make an effort to take your child to a football game or watch it on TV. If your child likes a movie that is based on a book, suggest he read the story first and then take him to see the movie. If your child is interested in buying an electronic device, ask him to first research different models and brands available and determine which would be a better buy.

Another way of helping your child develop an interest in reading is by providing him with books with which he can identify. At this age, your child might be more inclined to read books about "real-life" stories, especially those about pre-teen heroes or heroines who are going through similar problems and issues.

When a person shares their enthusiasm about a book they have read, it motivates others to want to read it as well. Therefore, one of the best ways to encourage your child to read is to model your own enjoyment of reading and share interesting parts of your own books with him.

Why Is It SO Important for Children to Read?   Students who consistently read books, novels, newspapers, magazines, or even look for information on the Internet often do well academically. Some of the academic benefits pre-teens obtain from reading are:

- Increased vocabulary in spelling, understanding of grammar, and speech construction.
- Improvement in the ability to understand complex ideas.

- Increased information and knowledge, beneficial in all courses.

- Improvement in writing skills by being exposed to various writing styles.

- Development of thoughts and opinions by reading and evaluating different points of views.

"Hey, it's helped me get this video game generation
interested in math..."

5. Emphasize the importance of math

By taking advanced math classes in grades 8 and 9, your child will have opportunity to take other advanced courses such as chemistry, physics, trigonometry, and calculus before finishing high school. Unfortunately, many middle school students do not take appropriate math classes, either because they are not enrolled in the correct courses or because they were not academically prepared to take these courses.

Help your child understand the importance of taking challenging math and science classes, as this will greatly increase his chances of being accepted to college. Also, share with your child that mathematics is used daily at most places of employment.

6. Explore College Access programs

College access programs such as Upward Bound, Educational Talent Search, GEAR UP, Advancement Via Individual Determination (AVID), Mathematics Engineering Science Achievement (MESA), Puente, and Early Academic Outreach Program (EAOP) are designed to help students develop strong academic skills and habits that will help prepare them for enrollment and success in college. These programs focus on developing important academic skills, such as working in groups, goal setting, time management, and writing. Most of these programs offer tutoring, mentoring, and organized visits to a number of college campuses. Ask your school staff if any of these programs are offered at your child's middle school.

7.   Encourage participation in extracurricular activities

As stated earlier, extracurricular activities add quality to life and expand a child's horizons both personally and academically. In middle school, there are many clubs, sports, music, and other activities from which to choose. Your child can participate in these activities in addition to his regular school work. Some examples include sports, band, volunteer work, and/or taking on a leadership role at school. There are many benefits to be gained from participating in extracurricular activities, such as making new friends, discovering new abilities, learning to work as part of a team, developing self-confidence, and reducing the risk of getting involved in gangs or using drugs and alcohol. This is a way for pre-teens to occupy themselves in activities that are both productive and safe.

8.   Start visiting colleges

As a family, think about starting to visit a variety of college campuses NOW with your child, even if it is just a short trip to the local community college. Remind your child that although he may think he will be the next professional athlete or music star, the reality is that there will be life after sports and/or the high school musical. Visiting a variety of college settings will provide your child a sense and feel of what life could look like for him in just a few short years.

9.   Promote a positive sense of self

A positive sense of self, also known as self-esteem, refers to how your child feels about himself. A child can create a self-image based on how proud he feels about his abilities.

When your child has high self-esteem, he has greater self-confidence and is able to make better decisions. He is also more likely to feel proud of his accomplishments, and will not be defeated easily by problems he may encounter.

It is very common for middle school students to feel insecure and judge themselves harshly. This preoccupation with insecurities can affect, among many things, your child's school performance. You can help him improve his self-concept by showing him respect and communicating effectively with him.

Since positive self-esteem is such an important factor in performing well academically, you as a parent should take advantage of every opportunity to help your child foster his self-confidence. You can start this by practicing effective parent/child communication.

10. Practicing effective parent-child communication

One of the best things you can do to foster positive self-esteem in your child is to communicate effectively with him, especially during the middle school years. Rather than speaking to him as you did when he was younger, it is important that you try to modify your language to address his new needs as a developing teenager. This is especially important for a child who might be facing unfamiliar situations at school and with his peer group.

Teach your child that effective communication consists of not only speaking, but more importantly, of knowing how to listen. A person who knows how to listen shows a true interest in what the other person is saying.

The final important component of effective communication is nonverbal communication. This consists of messages we transmit through body language, such as facial expressions, gestures, posture, eye contact, etc. Try your very best to be aware of the messages your body language might be sending to your child in addition to the words that you choose.

Tips to Help Raise Your Pre-Teen's Self-Esteem

When your teen wants to talk to you . . .

- Stop whatever you are doing. Turn off the TV. Put down the book you are reading. Give him your undivided attention.
- Be aware of your nonverbal communication and the messages it sends.
- Try not to give him input while he is talking, unless he requests it.
- Try not to bring up past problems or offer solutions right away.

FINAL REMINDERS TO ENSURE YOUR CHILD'S SUCCESS IN MIDDLE SCHOOL

- Confirm that your child is enrolled in college preparatory classes by speaking with his school counselor.
- Attend all parent nights and meetings at school to become informed of different programs and services that may benefit your child.

- Monitor your child's academic progress to ensure he is getting good grades. If your child is not meeting grade-level standards, meet with the school counselor and teachers to determine what steps you can take to help him improve.

- Continually talk to your child about going to college, not as a possibility, but as a true expectation.

- Encourage your child to talk with college students and others in his life to learn about experiences in college.

Remember: The greater parental involvement you have in the education and development of your child in middle school, the more academically prepared he will be for the critical next step to college—going to high school!

Chapter 4

The Critical High School Years

"A dream doesn't become a reality through magic, it takes sweat, determination and hard work."
—Colin Powell, former U.S. Secretary of State

High school at last! It is now finally time to let your guard down and allow your child to lead the way, right? Wrong!

As tempting as it sounds to allow your child to run the show with his educational future, the costs of letting that happen can be extremely high. Your teenager at this age believes that she knows much more than her parents do, but deep down, she still wants you to guide her. And for the college-going preparation process that lies ahead, she will need a great deal of guidance from you, whether she likes it or not. As mentioned in Chapter 1, children whose parents attended college are eight times more likely to complete a college education themselves (Source: Harvard University). This reality alone speaks volumes for the importance of parental involvement at this stage in your child's education.

Helping your child achieve a successful and rewarding high school experience requires your time, dedication, and careful planning, but it will be well worth the effort. The better prepared your child is academically upon high school graduation, the more options she will have in choosing a college and entering a fulfilling career.

A Parent Timeline by High School Grade Level is located in the Appendix section of this book.

HELPING YOUR CHILD ACHIEVE A POSITIVE HIGH SCHOOL EXPERIENCE

1. TALK to your child about her fears and excitement about going to high school

Similar to the transition from elementary to middle school, the transition from middle school to high school is often a time of emotional, physical, and academic stress. Your support and involvement are essential at this stage of your child's personal and academic development. Discuss with your child the concerns she has before starting high school. Your child may have concerns about the new environment, whether she will have classes with her friends or not, and the increased workload that her classes might bring. The more you can listen and engage with your child about this new transition, the more likely her fears will decrease over time.

2. LEARN about the course options that will be offered at her high school

Most high schools in California offer several categories of courses to students, depending on student needs and their plans for the future. The large variety of course offerings at the high school level might seem overwhelming at first, but discussing them often with your child will give her the confidence she needs to choose the classes she wishes to pursue.

The high school course options that you and your child should be able to choose from include:

Basic/Remedial

These courses are for students who need to improve their academic performance at grade level before they can move up to the more traditional pattern of courses.

Career and Technical Education Courses (CTE)

Career and technical education courses focus on work-related training that prepares students for a wide range of careers and further educational opportunities.

College Preparation (CP)

These courses will prepare students for the A-G requirements at the UC system, the CSU System, and private colleges and universities.

Advanced Placement (AP)/Honors

These courses are more challenging to students, and are accompanied by national tests that, depending on the results, can lead to college credits. All AP courses also count toward CSU and UC admissions and can be scored on a 5.0 GPA scale.

International Baccalaureate (IB)

IB courses have gained popularity due to their high standards and emphasis on creative and critical thinking. In IB courses, students are responsible for their own learning, choosing topics and devising their own projects, while teachers act more as supervisors or mentors than sources of facts. IB courses emphasize research and encourage students to learn from their peers, with students actively critiquing one another's work.

Concurrent Enrollment

Some high school districts partner with local community colleges and/or four year universities to allow students to enroll in a college course and receive high school credit at the same time. Some of these courses are held on the high school campus, and some on the college campus. These courses are beneficial in that they allow a student to earn college credit while still in high school.

Online College Courses

Online courses are an excellent way for your child to earn both high school and college credit. Your child's high school counselor will know which courses will meet the approval of the high school.

3.   Explore the high school in the spring of your child's 8th grade year.

A positive transition to high school is critical because the courses your child will complete will count toward her college admissions requirements. Many high schools host orientation programs for incoming freshmen students, often held in the spring of the students' 8th grade year. It is important to attend these orientations to help you answer the following questions:

- Is there a transition program for incoming 9th grade students (freshmen)?
- Is there a tour of the high school available to both parents and students?
- What course options does the high school provide to its freshmen students? How are students tested and placed into math and English courses?
- What are some of the elective courses offered to students?
- Are counselors available in the spring of the 8th grade year to help students select their course schedules?
- Can parents volunteer at the school?
- What is the school's safety policy?

- What extracurricular activities, music, art, and/or sporting activities are available at this high school?
- Does the school utilize a daily electronic bulletin to communicate with parents?
- Does the school have an anti-drugs/anti-drinking program that exposes the dangers of these substances to students?
- Does the school have a bullying prevention program?

4. Schedule a meeting with the high school counselor

At this stage in his education, it is critically important that your child take the right classes that will prepare him for high school graduation and college admission. You will want to closely monitor the courses your child is enrolled in each semester, and make sure he is enrolled in a college preparation track.

Questions that parents should ask the school counselor about course placement:

- Are my child's classes considered college prep courses?
- Is my child taking math classes that will prepare her to fulfill the requirements for college admissions?
- What electives do you recommend for students who plan on going to college?
- What activities can my child do at home or during the summer to prepare for college?
- How often are students graded? Every quarter, trimester, or semester?
- Is the grade point average (GPA) weighted (5.0) with Advanced Placement (AP) and/ or Honors classes worth more?
- Does my child's transcript include a profile with records of attendance, community service, a list of honors, and AP classes?
- Does my child's transcript include a school profile? (A school profile is a demographic record of the student population, AP/Honors classes offered, and other pertinent information that is usually required by college admissions officers.)
- Are there academic support or college access programs available on campus? How can I enroll my child in these programs?
- What classes could my child take if the ones that he is currently taking seem too easy and it appears that she has lost interest in them?

- Does the school offer a tutoring program?
- What other school programs can help my child maintain or improve her academic performance?
- When are the parent information nights scheduled?
- When are the teacher conferences scheduled?

5. LEARN about "A-G courses" required for college admissions

As stated in Chapter 3, the "A-G" courses are the required courses that high school students must take in order to gain admission to the CSU or UC systems in California. The bulk of A-G courses begin in high school, so this is the critical time for your child to enroll in and succeed in these courses. If your child plans to apply to a four-year college or university directly out of high school, request a copy of your child's class schedule each semester to ensure that she is taking the appropriate A-G courses. Many high schools have online websites (ARIES SIS) where parents can log into their child's records and ensure they are enrolled in the appropriate courses for four-year college admissions.

"A-G" Requirements by Subject Area

- **History/social science ("a")**—Two years, including one year of world history, cultures, and historical geography and one year of U.S. history, or one-half year of U.S. history and one-half year of American government or civics.
- **English ("b")**—Four years of college preparatory English that includes frequent and regular writing, reading of classic and modern literature, and practice listening and speaking.
- **Mathematics ("c")**—Three years of college-preparatory mathematics that include the topics covered in elementary and advanced algebra and two- and three-dimensional geometry.
- **Laboratory science ("d")**—Two years of laboratory science providing fundamental knowledge in at least two of the three disciplines of biology, chemistry, and physics.
- **Language other than English ("e")**—Two years of the same language other than English or equivalent to the second-level of high school instruction.
- **Visual and performing arts ("f")**—One year, including dance, drama/theater, music, or visual art.

- **College-preparatory elective ("g")**—One year chosen from the "a-g" courses beyond those used to satisfy the requirements above, or courses that have been approved solely for use as "g" electives.

6. ENCOURAGE participation in extracurricular activities

Grades and test scores are not the only requirements for college admission. Most colleges are looking for well-rounded students who have taken initiative and have participated in several activities, including sports teams, musical events, and clubs.

Admissions officers at UC and CSU campuses are especially looking for students who take on leadership roles with their teams and clubs. If your child excels in a sport and/or possesses a special talent, then encourage her to take the next step toward continuing to grow in her talent.

Also important is your child's participation in one or more of the college access programs already mentioned in Chapter 3. College access programs such as Upward Bound, Educational Talent Search, GEAR UP, AVID, MESA, Puente, Early Academic Outreach, and others help students develop the strong academic skills and habits that help increase their possibilities of graduating from college, and often can give them extra points on college and scholarship applications.

7. Encourage paid or volunteer work

If your child is not interested in extracurricular activities at her high school, perhaps you can encourage her to get a part-time job or volunteer work to give her some critical work experience along with some extra spending money. However, if she is involved in sports or extracurricular activities, she should not have a job during the school year due to homework loads and demands of non-academic activities. In this case, a summer job or internship would be a great way for your child to gain valuable work experience and perhaps allow her to explore a variety of possible career areas of interest.

8. LEARN the testing lingo!

You and your high school student will be bombarded with new phrases and acronyms that will be very important for you to understand. Some of the most confusing words in high school are the acronyms for the following tests that are required for high school graduation and/or college admission. Additional information about specific college admission tests will be covered in Chapter 8 on freshmen college admission. Tests you and your child will encounter are:

ACT

Taken during the junior or senior year, the ACT focuses on achievement rather than aptitude. Questions are drawn from content material covered in the high school curriculum. The ACT consists of four required sections and one optional section:

- English
- Math
- Reading
- Science
- Writing (optional)

The ACT takes about three hours to complete and students receive a score for each section. The scoring ranges from a low of 1 to a high of 36. Only about one out of every 5,000 students who take the ACT earns a composite score of 36. The writing part of the ACT (which is optional) measures skill in planning and writing a short essay. The CSU system does not require the score from the writing test for admission purposes, but the UC system does.

PSAT/NMSQT (Preliminary SAT/National Merit Scholarship Qualifying Test)

The PSAT is an assessment of reading, writing, and mathematical ability designed to give students the chance to become eligible for the National Merit Scholarship and compete for other scholarships. Students usually take the PSAT in their sophomore or junior year and the test is administered only once a year in October. Additionally, the PSAT is an opportunity for students to practice for the SAT.

SAT (Scholastic Assessment Test)

The SAT test is widely used as a college entrance examination by many colleges and universities. The SAT assesses how well students analyze and solve problems—which are skills they will need in college. The SAT is comprised of three (3) sections:

- Evidence-Based Reading and Writing
- Mathematics
- Essay (optional)*

Students typically take the SAT during their 11th and 12th grade years. The approximate testing time for the SAT is about three hours, plus 50 minutes for the optional essay. Each section of the SAT is scored on a scale of 400 to 1600, including a 2 to 8 score on each of three dimensions for the optional essay. The resulting scores will be compared to state and national averages of seniors graduating from any public or private high school.

See www.khanacademy.org/sat for official SAT Preparation information

SAT Subject Tests

The SAT subject tests are one-hour tests administered usually on the same test administration dates as the SAT (but the full SAT and SAT subject tests CANNOT be taken on the same day). The following SAT subject tests are offered five times per year:

- English: Literature
- History and Social Science: World History and U.S. History
- Languages: Chinese, French, German, Modern Hebrew, Italian, Japanese, Korean, Latin, and Spanish
- Math: Level I and II
- Science: Biology E (Ecological), Biology M (Molecular), Chemistry, and Physics

The CSU and UC systems no longer require the SAT subject tests, but they still strongly recommended that students continue to take them to remain competitive for college admissions.

ACT–ASPIRE Assessment

This test is a "pre-ACT" that serves as a powerful predictor of success on the ACT. The ASPIRE assessment test is typically administered in the fall of students' 10th grade year. Many high schools recognize the importance of this assessment for all students due to the fact that it focuses attention on both career preparation and improving academic achievement. The ASPIRE assessment covers the subject areas of English, Mathematics, Reading, and Science.

"Evidently, studying isn't one of the tasks
you perform when you're multitasking."

9. TEACH and reinforce study skills and time management daily

With all the events, tasks, and responsibilities that you have to juggle as a parent, you can see how helping to promote time management and study skills in your child will continue to benefit her throughout her entire educational lifetime and future career.

The first step is to help your child utilize easy time management tools. Require that your child use a weekly planner/calendar. Inexpensive planners can be purchased at any office supply store or may even be provided by your child's high school. The planner/calendar should be organized so that your child can record daily homework assignments each day in each subject area. Due dates of large projects and upcoming tests and quizzes should also be recorded. Your role as a parent is to check your child's planner frequently for completion, and to work with the teacher(s) to ensure that the assignment information is accurate.

In addition to daily class assignments, it is important to take a look at your child's total time commitment in all activities. At the beginning of the school year, sit down with your child and have her brainstorm everything she does each hour of the day for one week. This should include school, sleeping, homework, chores, sports practice, church, clubs, time spent with friends, playing outdoors, exercising, and free time. Then have her plug in all of these activities into her planner. Once all the activities and responsibilities are listed in the planner for the week, have her step back and take a look to see if everything fits. If not, work together with your child to prioritize what has to stay and what might need to be removed from her schedule. Decide together what is most important and devote the most time to those areas. Your child should get into the habit of updating her weekly schedule into her planner. Thus, when new activities and events come up, it will be easy to sit down together and look at the planner to see if these can fit into her schedule. (We have included a useful tool for this time planning exercise in the Appendix section of the book.)

10. Understand your child's natural daily rhythm for homework completion

First and foremost, determine what time of day your child will be the most productive doing homework. Imagine how you would feel if after working all day you had to come home to do one to three more hours of homework. When would be the best time for you to complete this work? Maybe your child works best in the morning after a good night's rest and can get up early to complete her homework before school; maybe she prefers to complete her homework in the afternoon after school. While some students can jump right into homework after school, others may need a break to eat or rest before diving back in. Work with your child to focus on completing her most difficult tasks first in order not to run out of energy working on other assignments before getting to the more difficult subject. Finally, allow your child to build incentives and rewards into her own homework schedule.

Rewards for homework could be based on time—such as a five-minute snack break after each thirty minutes of doing homework, or it could be based on the task. For example: Once the reading for science is complete, then she gets twenty minutes of free time before starting that essay for English class. This will help your child to see homework assignments as a series of small hills instead of one big mountain of homework. Make sure to eliminate as many distractions as possible by providing your child with a quiet and designated place for her to study. Good study habits lay the groundwork for successful work habits as adults.

11. Make homework completion a positive experience

Never Use Homework as a Punishment

Praise homework completion and maintain a positive and helpful attitude by avoiding any criticism. Be a good listener, and encourage your child to ask questions about subjects that she finds hard to understand.

Tutoring

Find someone to tutor your child if she is struggling in a particular course or subject in school. Ask about what tutoring services are available at the school. Many teachers are required to have structured study groups for students in their classes. Many students in the National Honor Society provide tutoring, and college students from local colleges may be available to provide after-school tutoring.

Model Positive Behavior

Children often model the behavior of their parents. For example, if your child sees you reading a book or the local newspaper, this might encourage her to read as well. Watch the news and ask your child for her opinion on world events and remind her that she will be voting soon and her opinion will matter.

12. Review test-taking skills

The most effective way for your child to prepare for class tests is by staying on top of her homework and paying attention in class. Students who complete their homework on a consistent basis are working toward an understanding of the content for the test. Consider the following to help your child prepare to be successful on her next test or exam:

- Have her mark the test date on her planner.

- Help your child set up a study schedule for when and how long she will study for the test.

- Encourage your child to schedule "periods of studying" to take place over the course of the week(s) before the test, not the night before. Cramming for a test does not result in a strong understanding of course contents and concepts.

- Encourage her to find out what format the test will be (multiple choice, essay, true/false, and/or fill in the blank, etc.). Knowing what types of questions are on the test will help her prepare more effectively.

- Talk about the test with your child. Ask about how she has prepared and worked in order to help alleviate any test anxiety. Do not appear to be worried or stressed about the test, that will just put more pressure on your child. Encourage your child to get a good night's sleep and eat well on the morning of the test.

- Remind your child to listen carefully to the instructions, read each question, and answer thoroughly. Tell her to make mental notes of key words such as "all," "never," "only," "always." These words can often indicate "trick" questions on a test.

- Celebrate success and discuss areas of improvement with your child after receiving test results.

- Set up a time to talk to your child's teacher to develop a plan to prepare for the next test if further assistance is needed.

13. LEARN about the best uses for technology

Your comfort level with today's technology may range from "computer guru" to "how does this thing turn on?" Regardless of your comfort level, helping your child navigate the changing world of technology may seem overwhelming. Even if she seems to be the computer expert teaching you how to use the latest and greatest gadget or piece of software, there is much you can still teach her. You have years of experience where you have learned many lessons that will help keep your child both safe and balanced in her use of technology.

The following lessons will help your child use technology in the most appropriate and safe manner:

Technology Lesson #1—Balance

There is little doubt that technology has helped improve our lives in many ways. That being said, technology can quickly overwhelm your child's life, consuming more time than it should. As a parent, you are in the ideal position to teach her proper balance. When you notice your child nervously checking her phone for text messages or social media updates, it is probably time sit down and have a talk about proper balance. Encourage her to engage in outdoor and/or face-to-face activities that may include sports or some other activity where she gets the social interaction and exercise she needs without being "plugged in" all the time.

Technology Lesson #2—Safety: Protecting Your Child's Reputation and Privacy

While technology has brought the world closer together, it has also brought potential dangers closer to your child. In dealing with social media, you must teach her how to protect her reputation and privacy.

Common pieces of information posted on social media sites by youth include: home/e-mail addresses; times when no one will be home photos; likes/dislikes; and interests. Obviously, much of this information could put your child in danger if the wrong person were to discover it. It would be wise to educate yourself and her about the privacy settings available on the social media sites she uses, and help your child to see the immense value of using them.

In order to further protect her, you should be included in her list of those individuals connected to her social media profile. Better yet, require her passwords so that you can log in to her site and review her communication with others occurring online. You can help your child see the dangers that posting pictures and commenting on social media sites poses to her reputation. In a matter of minutes, a posting can be viewed around the world (or at least around the school) and give an improper impression of your child that could impact her reputation for years to come. Encourage your child to regularly audit her social media contacts and postings by asking questions like: How well do I know this "friend" in real life? Do the photos I post reflect who I really am? Would I be embarrassed if someone like my parents, grandparents, or a future prospective employer were to see these photos? Teaching your child these skills will help keep her safer online and hopefully protect her reputation.

Technology Lesson #3—Use of Computer Tools for Class and Homework Assignments

The Internet can be a very useful tool in researching material for a class assignment or project. However, your child must be very careful in the manner that Internet-based information is included in her assignments. Websites such as blogs and forums tend to have subjective and opinionated information that should not be utilized in a research paper. Sites such as Wikipedia often have more reliable material but can occasionally be "hijacked" and include inaccurate or fraudulent information. Advise your child to be very cautious about using it as a source. More reliable information can be found on the Encyclopedia Britannica's fee-based website (http://www.britannica.com/), which has information contributed by experts in their fields. The Google Scholar site (http://scholar.google.com/) searches academic papers and publications and can help your child find information on any subject of choice. Finally, many libraries have online portals that allow your child to find or even read articles from a home computer.

Make sure that your child uses citations and quotes her sources. Talk to your child about plagiarism and make sure she knows that this is not only unethical and illegal, but it also prevents her from learning how to create and process her own words and thoughts, which is the real value of the assignment. Taking shortcuts will only keep her from developing the skills she needs for future academic success.

Helpful Software Tools: The most popular computer applications used in a high school setting are a collection of tools commonly called "Microsoft Office" and/or "Google Education." The software applications include word processing, spreadsheet, and presentation software. The word processing software is the application that most students use to write papers and essays.

Technology Lesson #4—Continuous Learning

Technology is constantly changing. Software programs such as Microsoft Windows and Excel can update several times a month. Other software may update several times in one day! In such an ever-changing environment, no one can really claim to know everything about technology. This may at first seem overwhelming to you. However, this can be viewed as an opportunity to teach your child the need for continuous learning. Most computer programs come with a help button. Often this includes step-by-step instructions on how to perform most tasks. If the built-in help features do not answer your questions, you will likely find the answer by simply typing your question into most Internet search engines. By teaching your child these computer skills, she will be able to navigate the continually changing technology environment for years to come.

14. Encourage public speaking opportunities

Public speaking is a valuable life skill. No matter the occupation your child chooses, the opportunity to speak in public could present itself at any time. Being able to use this skill efficiently can set your child apart from her peers in school and eventually in the career market. Many brilliant and talented professionals lack this skill, which can hinder their career advancement. With advice and practice, your child can become a skillful public speaker.

Public speaking in any form (prepared speech, interview, or otherwise) are performances and opportunities for success. Fear and nervousness are normal emotional responses that can actually aid the speaker. Emphasize to your child that nothing feels as empowering as commanding an audience!

15. Teach your child stress management tools

In today's competitive world of college admissions, it is no surprise that students and their parents are experiencing the pressure of more demanding classes, increased homework load, more stress surrounding college admission applications, as well as high-stakes admissions testing. However, you can suggest and personally model many stress-management tools for your child, which can reduce the anxiety-related demands of high school and increase academic productivity. Stress management tips for your child include:

- Get and stay organized: Keep your backpack and study area organized so it is clutter-free and accessible.

- Prioritize: Use a planner/calendar to keep track of academic deadlines and all extra-curricular activities. Avoid procrastination, it only creates more anxiety!

- Stay rested: Adequate sleep is crucial to balancing a healthy lifestyle. Young people devote less time to sleep as they age, and when you sacrifice sleep it has a negative impact on daily academic performance. When developing your weekly schedule, make sure that at least eight to nine hours of sleep is included each night. You may think you can make up hours on the weekend, but you may have also scheduled the weekends full with additional activities, work, and friends.

- Eliminate distractions: Turn off your cell phone, laptop, iPad, video games, and TV when studying.

- Practice healthy stress relief: Use healthy coping mechanisms such as exercise, meditation, or laughing with your friends. Students (and adults) literally stop breathing when stressed! Take a few moments during a study session or exam and breathe deeply to self-calm.

- Avoid over-scheduling: Be mindful of all of the pressures you may be experiencing and try not to push yourself to do too much. There are only twenty-four hours in the day so use them wisely.

16. Attend parent information nights and teacher conferences

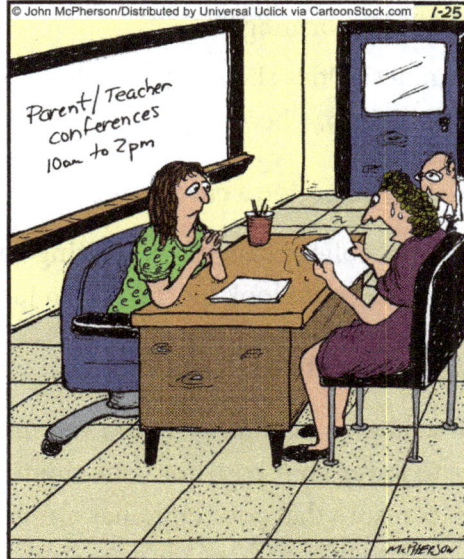

"What do you mean he got a C-minus on his report! I was up all night writing that thing!"

At the teacher conferences, ask your child's teachers similar questions to the ones you asked in middle school. Some examples are:

- I am very interested in tracking my child's academic progress. How can I stay informed?

- In what areas are my child having difficulty with in your class? How can we help her at home?

- Have you noticed any learning problems in my child? If so, what can I do to request an evaluation and additional support?

- When is the best time and means to contact you?

- How is she doing in relation to the rest of the class?

- How often are tests given to students in your class? How is my child doing on tests and quizzes?

- What will my child be working on this year?

- Is my child above, right at, or below her academic level?

- Approximately how much time should my child spend doing homework each day? What can I do to help her?

- Could you show me sample work that corresponds to my child's grade level to demonstrate how she should be performing?

- How are my child's grades? Does she need extra help? Does the school offer tutoring or other similar services? If so, when?

17. Continue to VISIT a variety of college campuses

Continue visiting a variety of college campuses. Visiting college campuses will give your child a sense and a feel of what life could look like for her in just a few short years.

18. Start or continue SAVING for college costs

Starting early to save for college is very important. Even if you have not started saving for college yet, there is still time to lower your costs for your child's college education through the following easy mechanisms to ensure that your child has ample funding for college.

- Learn about the tax advantages of state college savings plans such as 529 college savings plans and prepaid tuition plans at https://www.scholarshare.com.

- Read "Saving Early = Saving Smart!" at https://studentaid.ed.gov/sites/default/files/saving-early.pdf. This website explains in detail why it is never too early to save money for college and how to use such resources as college savings plans and federal student aid.

- Use FAFSA4caster at http://www.FAFSA4caster.ed.gov to find out how much federal student aid your child might be eligible to receive. This information should help you plan ahead. (We will cover the many forms of financial aid available in Chapter 10.)

19. Set realistic expectations about playing sports in college

If your child plays sports in high school and desires to continue to play sports in college, the first place to start is with a reality check. If your child has her heart set on playing Division I college sports, be sure to make her aware of the following: The reality is that a very low percentage of high school players nationwide end up playing sports in college. In 2013–14, the breakdown of high school athletes accepted to play at the college level was the following (from www.scholarshipstats.com).

- Basketball—5.9 percent of high school boys and 6.3 percent of high school girls.
- Soccer—8.9 percent of high school boys and 9.6 percent of high school girls.
- Baseball—11.2 percent of high school boys.
- Softball—7.8 percent of high school girls.
- Football—7.8 percent of high school boys.

These are not great odds. If your child is still interested in pursuing sports in college, consider guiding your child in the following ways, starting no later than your child's junior year:

- Obtain a realistic assessment of your son/daughter's athletic talent. This talent assessment will help you determine the appropriate level of play for your son/daughter at the college level. Do not rule out NAIA or NCAA Division II and III colleges if they can help your child attain his/her academic goals. Casting a wide net will improve your child's chance of being successfully recruited.

- Have a realistic expectation with respect to available athletic scholarship money. In addition to athletic scholarships, many colleges offer other types of financial assistance and the pool of available money may be substantially increased if your child has strong academic grades and test scores.

- Some colleges do not offer athletics scholarships, or need to allocate scarce scholarship money to more players than their program is funded to carry. It is not uncommon in smaller schools, or less prominent sports programs at larger schools, for scholarships to cover only a portion of the costs associated with attending college. However, your child can supplement his/her total financial package through other forms of financial aid such as academic or grants, scholarships, and/or student loans.

Tips If Your Child Has an Interest in Playing a Sport at the College Level

- Talk to your child's high school coach for advice.
- Ask for a realistic assessment of your child's appropriate next level of play.
- Gauge the high school coach's interest in promoting your child to college scouts and coaches.
- Ask if the coach is willing to take the next step of reaching out to college coaches on behalf of your child.
- Have child attend off-season tournaments for exposure.
- Post a highlight package on YouTube and let college coaches know how to find it by including the full URL in your correspondence.
- Shoot a short three-minute DVD with sports highlights that show off your child's athletic ability and skills.
- Include your contact information in the video.

IMPORTANT NEXT STEPS IN COLLEGE AND CAREER PREPARATION

Your high school student is going to be very busy with her academic studies and activities while in high school. However, it is critically important that she also devote a good amount of time to researching and exploring possible careers that might interest her. Thankfully, most students find that this exercise can be an enjoyable part of their high school experience. In the next chapter, we will give you the steps needed to point your child in the right direction for planning the future career of her dreams.

Chapter 5

The Importance of Career Exploration

"All our dreams can come true,
if we have the courage to pursue them"
—Walt Disney

While there are many outstanding experts in the field of career exploration, Sir Ken Robinson has been the most highly regarded leader in career development for more than thirty years. Sir Robinson strongly believes that it is important for children to get in touch with their natural abilities in order to find meaning in their lives. He believes that all children are born with natural abilities and talents, yet most of them lose touch with these special talents as they grow up, sometimes, quite sadly, through the efforts of our formalized educational system.

Sir Robinson observes that children often grow up not knowing who they are and what they are capable of doing, because they never have a chance to discover and connect with their true talents and abilities. In order to change this situation, Sir Robinson urges parents to think differently about their children's lives, their unique learning styles, and their unique talent

There are thousands of highly successful adults earning a great living by using their unique talents. These adults were fortunate to have discovered the one or two talents that they naturally do well, and found achievement and satisfaction in doing them. Sir Robinson calls this meeting point between natural talent and satisfaction "The Element," and believes this is essential to an individual's well-being and ultimate success.

At times, our educational system overvalues the core academic subjects of math, science, and language skills at the expense of creative thinking skills. Our system often rewards finding the "right" answers rather than using one's imagination or unique intelligence. More emphasis is often placed on standardized testing rather than on developing students' natural abilities and enabling them to make their unique way in the world. It is very important for parents to realize this disconnect and encourage their children to find their unique selves. This self-exploration can begin as early as elementary school and should continue into high school.

Parent help is critical. Research demonstrates that parents have the greatest influence on their children's educational and career choices (Guerra and Braungart-Ricker 1999). The reasons for this include:

- Parents know their children better than anyone else.
- Parents have the most interest in helping their children choose a rewarding and fulfilling career.
- Parents know that their children's future is too important to be left to luck or chance.

It is also important for parents to realize that children will sometimes choose careers for what could be the wrong reasons:

- Some children focus on only what they have grown up around and only consider careers similar to their parents.
- Some children choose a career path based only on its salary.

- Some individuals "fall into" a career because they started a job and it was just easier to stay in it.

Help your child discover his unique interests and skills. Since your child will be more successful and satisfied with his career choice if the career is based on his interests and skills, your first step is to help your child identify possible career paths that match his unique interests and skills.

This chapter will focus on four activities that you as a parent can do with your child to help guide him down the path of his career exploration journey.

Activity #1—Ask Questions

Ask your child the following questions to assist him in determining what his interests are:

- What extracurricular activities do you enjoy the most?
- What do you like to do with your friends?
- What special skills do you think you have?
- What have you done that you are most proud of?
- What is your favorite subject in school?
- What activities interest you the most?

Take notice of the activities, books, movies, and television shows your child likes. Check out the websites he visits while online, and how he uses his free time. Once you have helped your child identify some of his interests, you may suggest he engage in activities that nurture those interests. For example:

If your child has an interest in animals, he might want to:

- Join a 4-H club
- Volunteer at a local veterinary clinic
- Walk or care for a neighbor's dog

If your child has an interest in art, he might want to:

- Design a personal website
- Make birthday or holiday cards for relatives and friends
- Create graphics for the school newsletter

If your child likes to help people, he might want to:

- Apply to be a summer camp counselor

- Babysit for a friend or relative

- Teach a younger child to read

If your child likes to build or repair things, he might want to:

- Build a radio or computer from a kit

- Take apart an appliance and put it back together

- Design and build a bird house

If your child likes to play sports, he might want to:

- Play on a sports team

- Assist a coach

- Umpire or referee community games

Activity #2—Explain How Interests Can Match Potential Careers

Begin by explaining how your child's likes and interests could match potential careers. For example:

- If your child likes art: Discuss how art is used to design houses, clothing, magazine ads, movie sets, and even toys. Explain that art is also used to draw cartoons, arrange flowers, and take photos for magazines and books.

- If your child likes to be outdoors: Discuss how careers in this field usually involve working outside such as landscaping, architecture, construction, forestry, archaeology, construction, marine biology, or commercial fishing.

- If your child likes to help people: Talk about different ways he can do that as part of being a nurse, doctor, athletic trainer, paramedic, family counselor, or child care worker.

- If your child loves math: Talk with him about the possibility of becoming an accountant, a computer programmer, engineer, or statistician. You should also remind your child that almost all careers require the use of basic math, an important skill to possess.

- If your child likes to keep others safe: Talk to him about a career as a police officer, forensic scientist, detective, investigator, parole officer, security guard, or firefighter.

Activity #3—Go Online for Career Search Exercises

The California Career Zone is a free website from the California Career Resource Network; it is designed to help middle and high school students learn more about themselves. This site provides students with insight about their interests, strengths, values, and skills, and then matches them with a number of potential career choices. The site below can be found at www.cacareerzone.com.

Figure 6   California Career Zone

Here are the seven steps needed to complete the activities on the California Career Zone site:

Step 1—Create a personal portfolio

Go to http://www.cacareerzone.org and have your child create a personal portfolio by clicking on "Register Now" in the middle of the page. Students will be asked to create a username, password, and provide their zip code. Students also may provide an e-mail address so that the password can be reset if it is forgotten.

Step 2—Have your child take a quick quiz about how occupations relate to his interests and skills

Direct your child to sign in and click the "Assess Yourself " link. Click the first option listed, "Quick Assessment" (shown in the following figure). After reading through the definitions for each occupation area, have your child complete the Quick Assessment in order to receive his personalized "code."

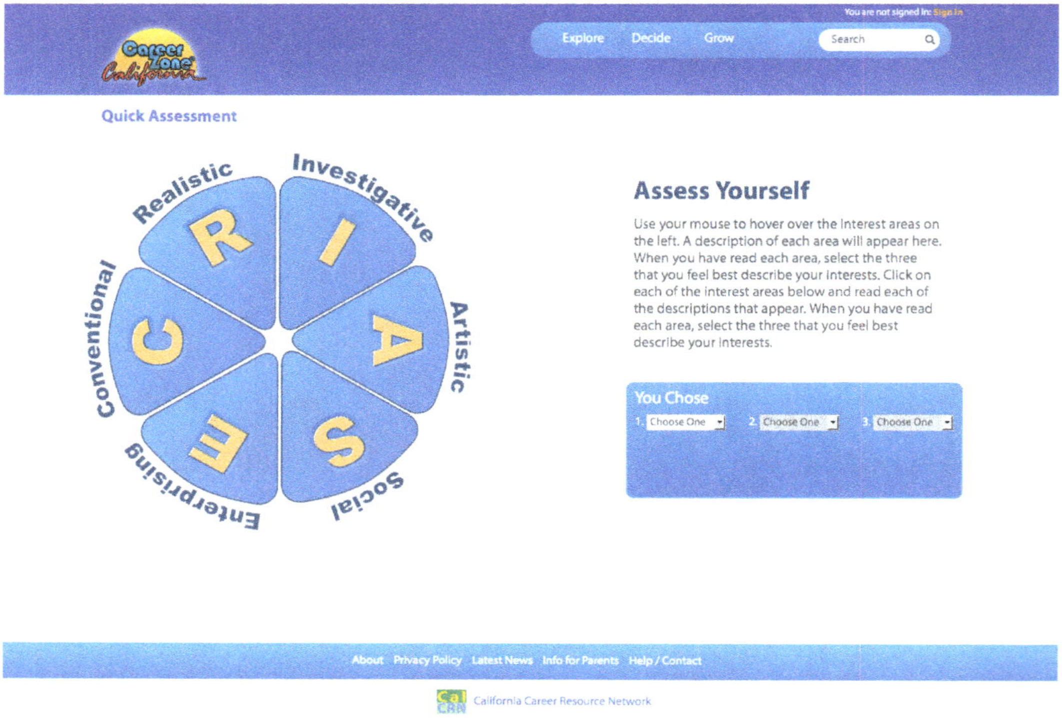

Figure 7   California Career Zone Assessment Quiz

There are six personality types known as the "Holland Code" types—the most widely used tool in the career exploration field. The code categories are:

1. Realistic
2. Investigative
3. Artistic
4. Social
5. Enterprising
6. Conventional

The Holland Code is based on the following three essential principles

1. Most people fall into one of the six general personality types listed earlier.

2. People of the same personality type tend to "hang out together." For example, artistic people are attracted to making friends and working with other similar artistic people.

3. People of the same personality type who work together create a work environment that fits that personality type. For example, when artistic people work together, they create a work environment that rewards creative thinking and behavior—which is an artistic environment.

"I imagine you're interested in one of the more highly visible occupations?"

The Holland Code personality types

- **Realistic**—Realistic people are usually assertive and competitive, and are interested in activities requiring motor coordination, skill, and strength. People with a realistic orientation usually prefer to work a problem through by doing something, rather than talking about it, or sitting and thinking about it. They like concrete approaches to problem solving, rather than abstract theory. They tend to be interested in scientific or mechanical rather than cultural and aesthetic areas. They like to work with THINGS.

- **Investigative**—Investigative people like to think and observe rather than act, to organize and understand information rather than to persuade. They tend to prefer individual rather than people-oriented activities. They like to work with DATA.

- **Artistic**—Artistic people are usually creative, open, inventive, original, perceptive, sensitive, independent, and emotional. They do not like structure and rules, like tasks involving people or physical skills, and are more likely to express their emotions than others. They like to think, organize, and understand artistic and cultural areas. They like to work with IDEAS and THINGS.

- **Social**—Social people seem to satisfy their needs through teaching or helping situations. They are different than Realistic and Investigative Types because they are drawn more to seek close relationships with other people and are less apt to want to be really intellectual or physical. They like to work with PEOPLE.

- **Enterprising**—Enterprising people are good talkers, and use this skill to lead or persuade others. They also value reputation, power, money, and status, and will usually go after it. They like to work with PEOPLE and DATA.

- **Conventional**—Conventional people like rules and regulations and emphasize self-control. They like structure and order, and dislike unstructured or unclear work and interpersonal situations. They place value on reputation, power, or status. They like to work with DATA.

Step 3—Create a record of interesting occupations

Now have your child list the occupations identified from his personalized Holland Code that he finds most interesting in a personal notebook or journal.

Some example codes are:

- ASE—Music director
- CEI—Customs inspector
- IES—Criminologist
- SAE—Art teacher

(College majors sorted by Holland Codes can be found in the Appendix)

Step 4—Reassess his interests

Have your child complete the Interest Profiler found on the "Assess Yourself " link on the website. Did your child's Holland Code end up being the same or similar to the ones from his Quick Assessment results (Step 2)? Have your child write down all the career options that interest him in his notebook.

Step 5—Discover his skills and the jobs that match those skills

Have your child complete the Skills Profiler which can be found on the "Assess Yourself" link. The Skills Profiler will help your child explore occupations that require the skills he may already possess. Have your child write the answers to the following in his notebook:

My Top 3 Skills   The Top 3 Jobs That Match My Skills

_____

_____

_____

Step 6—Work importance profiler

After completing the first three assessments (Quick, Interests, and Skills Profiler), your child is ready to complete the work importance profiler. The results from this work assessment will provide your child with a list of jobs that match his "ideal" work environment/setting. The results will also include specific information on careers, employment trends, salaries, growing and declining fields, job outlook, and education and training opportunities.

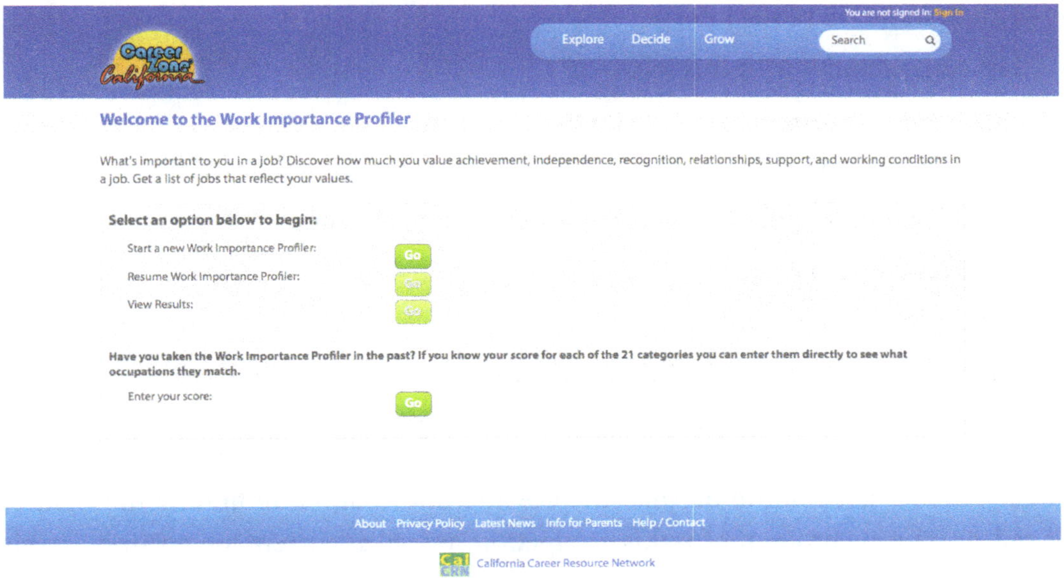

Figure 8   California Career Zone Work Importance Profiler

The work importance profiler has three important components that will help your child identify his "best fit" work environment.

Component one—"The ideal job"

Have your child answer the twenty-one statements and score them with a one to five score (with one as highest and five as lowest) based on his ideal job description: For example "For my ideal job it is important that I can do things for other people."

Component two—Work preference questions

Have your child answer yes or no to statements regarding ideal job activities. For example: The statement will say "In my ideal job, it is important that I be busy all of the time" and then your child must answer either yes or no.

Component three—The Summary

This summary will provide your child with a list of his top work values, in order of importance. The summary will also provide your child with a list of jobs that strongly match his values, interests, skills, and preferences in a work setting. Most importantly, a specific list of jobs that best match your child's interest is just a click away, and he will be able to compare potential future careers side-by-side. The summary will give your child the following information about each listed job:

- Full description of the job
- His compatibility with this job
- What other names the job may go by
- What workers do daily in this job
- The education required to be hired for this job in the future
- The average salary
- Future employment outlook
- The industries that employ this occupation
- Common college majors to prepare for this career

Finally, the far left column on this site provides information on finding the right educational and/or training programs for this occupation, as well as current job postings in this field by city and state.

Step 7—Take notes!

Instruct your child to read the description on the website for each occupation and make a list of the skills or tasks that sound interesting to him. Have your child answer the following questions in his notebook:

- What skills do I already have from my list?
- What skills do I want to learn?
- What is the lowest education level I will need in order to enter this occupation/career?
- What is the highest education level I will need in order to enter this occupation/career?

The following table provides a few examples of potential careers and the college education that may be recommended or required for each career.

Two-Year College (Associate Degree)	Four-Year College (Bachelor's Degree)	More Than Four Years of College (Graduate Degree Required)
• Administrative assistant • Automotive mechanic • Cardiovascular technician • Commercial artist • Computer technician • Dental hygienist • Drafter • Engineering technician • Funeral director • Graphic director • Graphic designer • Heating, air-conditioning, and refrigeration technician • Hotel or restaurant manager • Medical laboratory technician • Medical record technician • Insurance agent • Registered nurse • Surgical technologist • Surveyor • Visual artist • Water and wastewater treatment plant operator	• Accountant • Computer systems analyst • Dietitian • Editor • Engineer • FBI Agent • Investment banker • Journalist • Medical illustrator • Pharmacist • Public relations specialist • Recreational therapist • Research assistant • Social worker • Teacher • Writer	• Architect • Biologist • Chiropractor • Dentist • Diplomat • Doctor • Economist • Geologist • Lawyer • Librarian • Management consultant • Paleontologist • Priest • Psychologist • Public policy analyst • Rabbi • Scientist • Sociologist • University professor • Veterinarian • Zoologist

Table 5   Careers and the College Education Needed

Activity #4—Reality Check

Now that your child has a list of possible careers that match his interests and skills, you can help him learn about the potential for earning a living in each of these careers. It is very important that parents help their children realize and understand that there can be a very large difference in salary levels between career choices.

Most students in high school do not spend any time thinking about rent, transportation, property taxes, food costs, utilities, or how much income will be needed to pay for these items and other costs of living. This next career exploration activity will help your child understand the reality of the future cost of living and focus on the question of: "Can I afford the lifestyle I want in the career area I am interested in?"

The free site at http://www.cacareerzone.org/budget/ is used by thousands of middle and high school students and their teachers every year. This site matches your child's desired lifestyle with a heavy dose of reality regarding the required education and training needed to obtain a career to help him achieve that lifestyle. This site has an online budgeting exercise that provides students with a glimpse into their future costs of living such as housing, utilities, food, and transportation. It takes cost of living information and compares it to an annual salary, summarizing what your child must earn in order to achieve and maintain his desired lifestyle. After completing this exercise to determine the annual salary required for the lifestyle he has chosen, your child can then begin to explore jobs and careers where he might earn the required salary.

Follow the steps below to help your child navigate through this enjoyable website.

Step 1: Go to http://www.cacareerzone.org/budget/

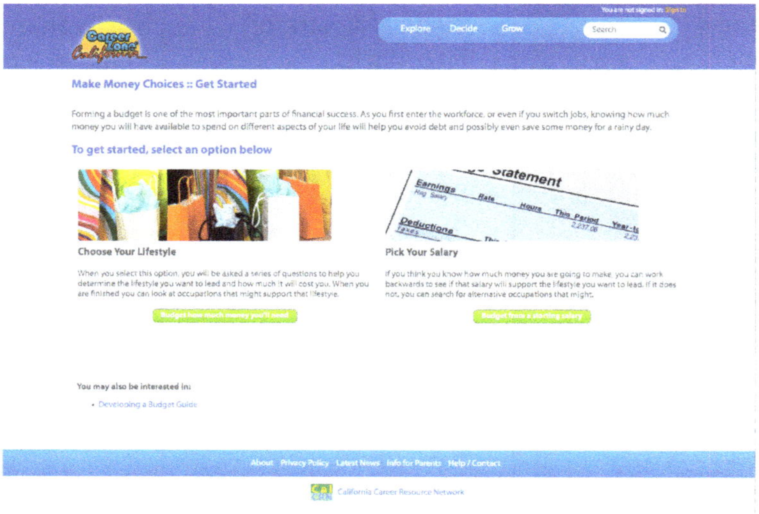

Figure 9   California Career Zone Lifestyle-Budget Exercise

Category	Your Selection	Expense
Housing		
Utilities/Phone		
Food		
Transportation		
Clothes		
Health Insurance		
Personal		
Entertainment		
Miscellaneous		
Savings		
Education		
Family Plan Additional Cost		
Total Monthly Expenses		
Annual Expenses		
Taxes		
Annual Salary Needed		

Table 6   Lifestyle-Budget Worksheet

Step 2: When the Living Space link opens, choose the California city your child hopes to live in.

Remind your child that the cost of living varies a great deal from city to city and ranges from very expensive to affordable. Have your child answer the following questions in his notebook:

What city did you choose to live in? Why did you choose this city?

Step 3: Have your child proceed with selecting his lifestyle choice by selecting a housing option.

Click the green arrow after your child makes his selection from each category. Have your child continue to go through each category and write down the dollar amount of his selections using the following format.

Notice as your child goes through the listed categories that each expense will appear in the "Expense" column in the cost calculator. Below the expense box will be a running balance. This balance is the total cost of all lifestyle selections your child has made so far.

Step 4: Click on the green arrow underneath "View Occupations."

The site will then give you a list of occupations that would meet your child's chosen lifestyle budget. If he clicks on each occupation listed, a wealth of information will be displayed, including:

- Information about the job
- What the job is also called
- What people do in this job
- Education needed
- Wages for 2013
- Outlook for the future for this occupation
- Common college majors to prepare for this job
- Interests of people who work in the occupation
- Work values of people who work in the occupation
- Things he would need to know to be successful at this job
- Things he would need to be able to DO to be successful at this job
- Industries that employ this occupation

Please note that the educational levels on this website range from a high school diploma to a professional degree. Have your child write down the occupations selected, and include the educational requirements, wages, and each job outlook in his notebook in the suggested format below.

Occupations	Educational Requirements	Wages	Job Outlook

Table 7 Occupations Worksheet

ADDITIONAL CAREER EXPLORATION ACTIVITIES FOR HIGH SCHOOL STUDENTS

Internships and/or Summer Jobs

High school students should plan on obtaining some type of related job experience. Your child might consider participating in one or more school-affiliated internships or jobs (paid or unpaid). As an intern, he can gain valuable work experience at businesses, government offices, and nonprofit agencies. Early work experience can pay off in the future.

Informational Interviews

One way to learn all about the ins and outs that come with a particular job or career is to actually speak to individuals already working in that occupation or career. While it might be awkward or difficult for your child to set up meetings with professionals in your community, there is a remarkable resource by the name of Roadtrip Nation. This organization literally goes "on the road" to interview various professionals about their career area, and makes these informational interviews accessible online. For a small fee, your student will have access to hundreds of personal interviews with professionals in the career areas in which he may be interested. The Roadtrip Nation site can be found at http://roadtripnation.com.

Figure 10   Roadtrip Nation Website

Note to Parents about the Importance of Career Exploration

Exploring careers early does not mean that these decisions are set in stone. It does mean that your child will most likely make better career decisions because he will more confidently move forward utilizing the foundation you provided for him during elementary, middle, and high school.

Early career development is important to open your child's eyes to the countless career paths and opportunities available to him. Career development is a life-long process and you should expect your child's plans to change often as he matures and gathers more information.

Finally, it is crucial to note that one of the top ten reasons students drop out of college is a lack of career focus (http://www.leavingacademia.com/top-reasons-to-leave/). *Finally, the longer a college student remains undecided regarding a career choice, the more likely he (and you) will need to spend additional years and money to earn a college degree.* Early career exploration is the key to career focus while also saving time plus thousands of dollars on your child's college education.

Once your child has a career area narrowed down, the next step will be to choose a college major that will best prepare him for the career of his choice.

Chapter 6

Choosing a College Major and Degree

"To guide someone to their future is more meaningful
if we don't try to dictate the journey"
—Louise Barbee, Author

In Chapter 5, you learned how to help your child research her interests and skills and make a list of possible career choices. Ideally, she should have a general idea of a career field of interest before starting to investigate potential college majors and degrees. This chapter will focus on helping your child select a college major and degree that will provide her the best preparation for her desired career(s).

CHOOSING A MAJOR

What is a major?

A "major" is a short term for the "major area of study" your child will focus on at the university or college she chooses. Major courses have a common theme and are geared toward preparing your child for specific educational and/or career areas.

Why is a major so important?

As we discussed in Chapter 5, the choice that your child makes about her major field of study is a key component of developing her career plan. Too many students choose major fields of study by default without giving the choice much consideration, at least with respect to the kinds of career options this choice will both create and eliminate.

Many high school seniors often put the most emphasis on the reputation of the colleges they attend, but employers are putting more emphasis on the student's major, their work experiences, and the skills required for the college degree that can be utilized in the workforce (From: Collegegrad.com, 2014).

In 2014, Collegegrad.com released the results of its survey on "What Employers Want Most in Hiring New College Grads." The results might surprise you. In order of importance, today's employers consider the following as the most important indicators when hiring recent college graduates:

#1—The student's major area of study (44 percent)

#2—The student's interviewing skills (18 percent)

#3—The student's internship/experience (17 percent)

#4—The college that the student graduated from (10 percent)

#5—Other miscellaneous qualifications (5 percent)

#6—The student's GPA (4 percent)

#7—The student's personal appearance (1 percent)

#8—The student's computer skills (1 percent)

As you can see from the list, it is critically important that your child conduct the research needed and seriously consider potential major/career areas before she even applies to college.

Can a major be changed?

Absolutely! Assure your child that it is perfectly OKAY if she is uncertain about the career or major area she wants to pursue right out of high school. Research has shown that up to 80 percent of entering college students admit that they are not certain what to major in, even if they have declared a major. Before college graduation, more than 50 percent of college students change their major at least once (Source: http://dus.psu.edu and http://nces.ed.gov/programs/coe/).

It is important to note that the most popular major in many colleges is "undeclared," which shows that making this life-changing decision is a complex step. By choosing "undeclared," your child can explore courses in a number of subject areas before deciding on the major that most interests her.

However, parents, please proceed here with caution. Because of the cost and time involved, it is very important that your child's decision of a major be made at least some time within her first two years of college. Every year that goes by means more time and money needed for completing her required degree or certificate.

Following are three exercises designed to help your child research majors based on the career areas she selected in Chapter 5, and eventually narrow her choices down to two to three majors that she can explore further, and discover those that will have the highest possibility of leading her to a fulfilling career.

Exercise #1—Helping your child match her personality to potential majors

In Chapter 5 your child discovered the Holland Code, a code that gives your child information about her unique personality type. Just as this code helped her in her career search, it can now help in researching major fields of study that will match her interests and skills.

For the first step in this exercise, direct your child to the following website: http://homeworktips.about.com/library/maj/bl_majors_quiz.htm

This website provides a fun and easy quiz adapted from Holland's career and interest survey to introduce your child to the types of questions she should be asking herself when choosing a major. After answering ten questions, your child will be given a list of suggested majors based on her personality type. Emphasize to your child that this is not an exhaustive list of potential majors, it is just a point from which she can begin her research. If possible, have her print the results and record any majors that appeal to her and at least one she is not familiar with.

On the results page, there will be a helpful list of potential majors grouped by Holland personality type. For example, if the first letter of your child's Holland code is "R," then she may be interested in the majors listed under the Realistic column. Again, it should be emphasized that this is not an exhaustive list of majors or degree programs, but can be used as a tool to help guide your child's research toward a potential major area of study. Please note that colleges and universities are constantly adding new majors to their course offerings. As new technology and career fields emerge, the types of majors available also will change.

Exercise #2—What can I do with a major in . . . ?

A favorite site of many career counselors and other educators is https://career.berkeley.edu/Major/Major.stm.

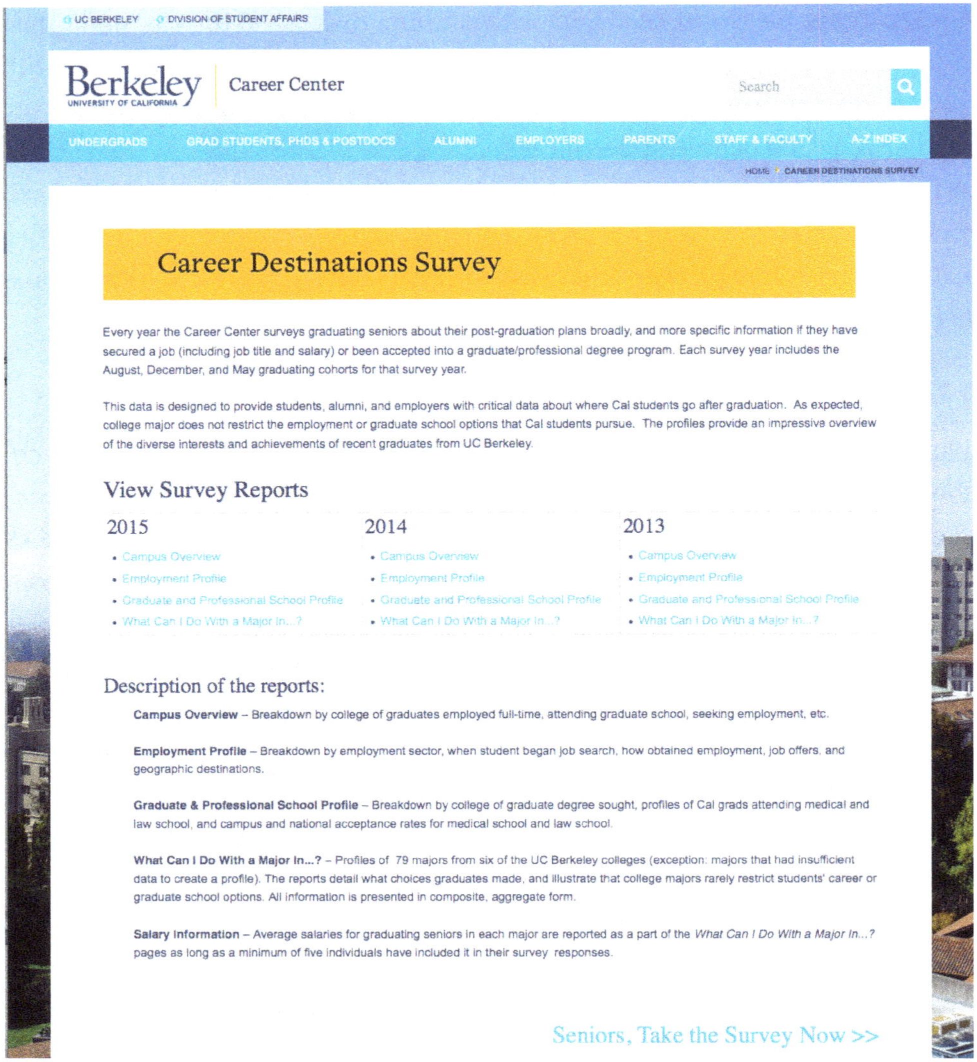

Figure 11   Career Destinations Survey: What Can I Do With a Major In . . . ?

This site will help your child answer the question: "What can I do with a major in . . .?" Your child fills in the blank. On this site your child will be able to enter any major of interest, do a quick search, and the site will provide detailed specifics about potential career paths that this major could lead to.

Exercise #3—Career path details

The Occupational Outlook Handbook is published annually by the U.S. Bureau of Labor Statistics and is available online at http://www.bls.gov/ooh/.

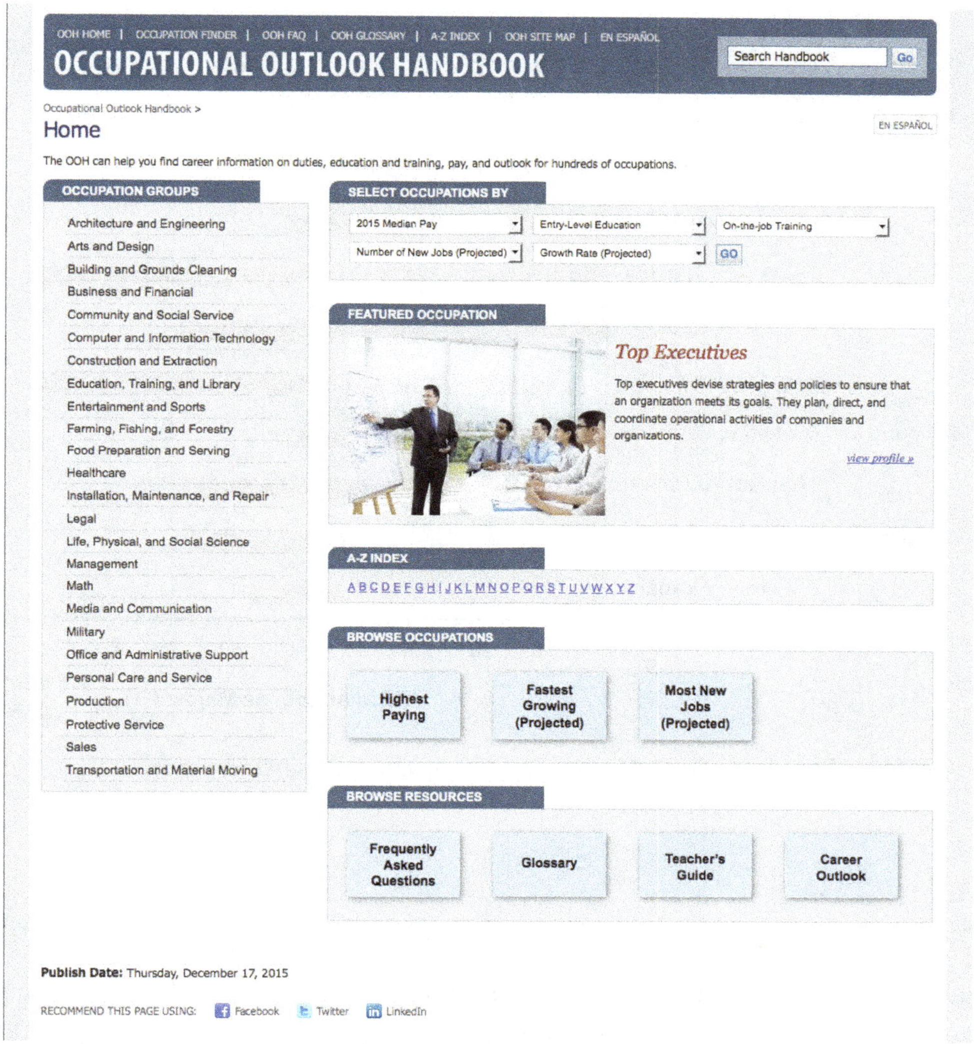

Figure 12   Occupational Outlook Handbook

This valuable website has a description for every career your child can imagine. Each job description covers information such as the training and education needed, earnings, expected job prospects, what workers do on the job, and working conditions.

What are the most popular majors?

Many parents and students want to know which majors are more popular than others. The following table provides information on the ten most popular majors nationwide in 2014.

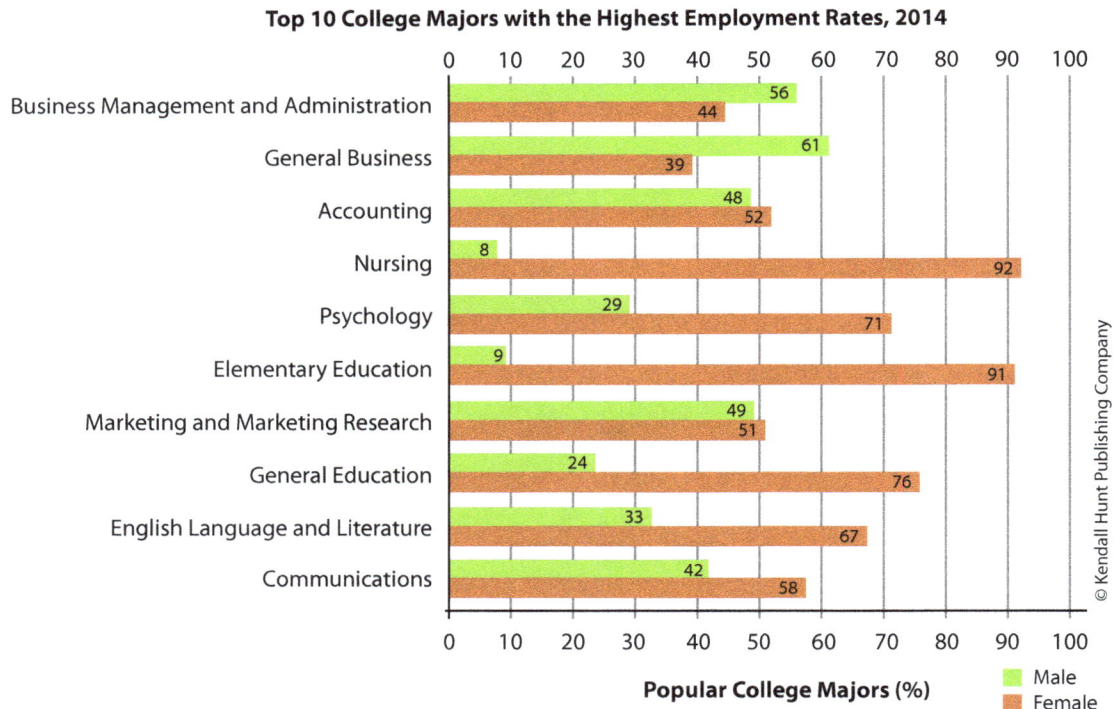

Top 10 College Majors with the Highest Employment Rates, 2014

Major	Male	Female
Business Management and Administration	56	44
General Business	61	39
Accounting	48	52
Nursing	8	92
Psychology	29	71
Elementary Education	9	91
Marketing and Marketing Research	49	51
General Education	24	76
English Language and Literature	33	67
Communications	42	58

Popular College Majors (%)

© Kendall Hunt Publishing Company

Table 8 Ten Most Popular College Majors, 2014. www.businessinsiders.com.

What majors are most likely going to lead to a job right out of college?

Because college requires such a large investment in time, energy, and money, many parents want to know which majors have the most likely chance of leading to a job right out of college. The top ten majors with the highest employment rates after college graduation in 2013 are shown in Table 9. Keep in mind however, your child should not choose a major field of study based strictly on her job prospects right after college. If a major field of study leads to a career that she is unhappy doing, she is not going to achieve the level of success or fulfillment she would if instead she studied for a career that matched her interests and personality.

Top 10 College Majors with the Highest Employment Rates, 2014

Major	Employment Rate (%)
Geological and Geophysical Engineering	100
Military Technologies	100
Pharmacology	100
School Counseling	100
Medical Assisting Services	99
Metallurgical Engineering	99
Treatment Therapy Professions	99
Agricultural Economics	98
Agriculture Production and Management	98
Atmospheric Sciences and Meteorology	98

© Kendall Hunt Publishing Company

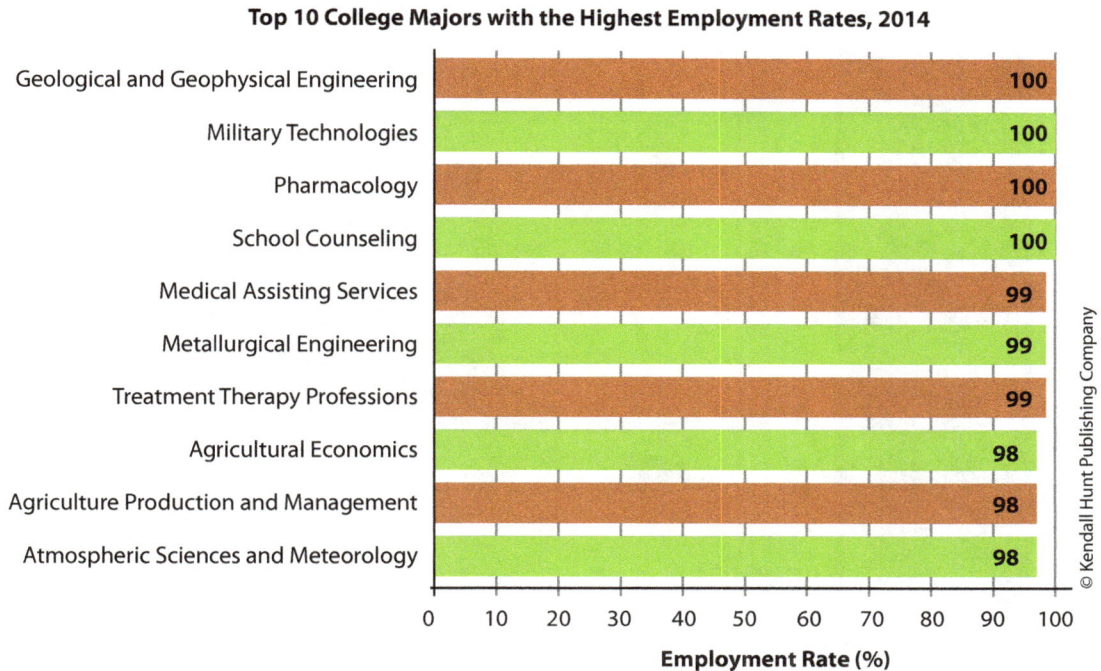

Table 9   Top 10 College Majors with the Highest Employment Rates, 2014. www.businessinsiders.com.

One important note—colleges and universities do not call majors the same thing. For example, at one college a major area may be titled "Geophysical Engineering" and at another college it might be called "Geotechnical Engineering," and at yet another college it might be called "Earth Science."

Which colleges/universities offer the major your child is interested in?

Once your child has decided which major area she wants to study, the next step is to find out which colleges offer that major area of study, and which degrees can be earned while studying that major.

For a complete list of majors by public school system in California, the very best site to use is: http://www2.assist.org/exploring-majors/Welcome.do.

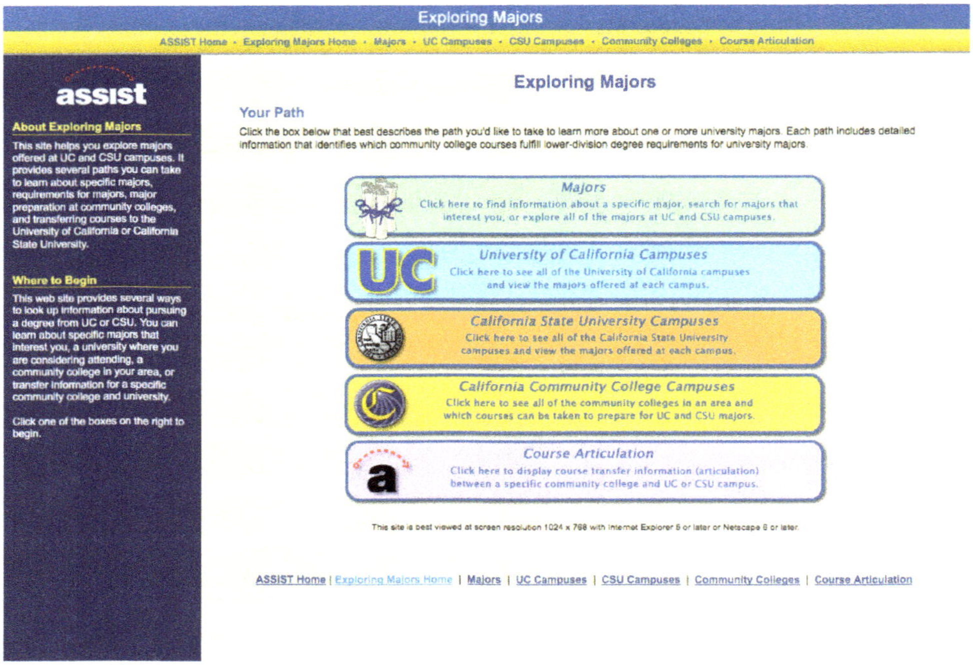

Figure 13   Exploring College Majors

This valuable site provides information on all the public four-year institutions in California. By using this site, your child can type in the name of the major she is interested in and the site will provide information on all institutions in California that offer that major area of study. In addition, your child can click on the name of any institution on the map of colleges provided, and a list of available majors offered on that specific campus will appear.

CHOOSING A DEGREE

Now that your child has researched majors that match her interests, and has located colleges that offer these majors, it is time to decide on what type of "degree" to pursue.

What is a degree?

A degree is the certificate awarded to a student who has completed a designated number of courses in a major field of study. Descriptions of the most common degrees offered at California colleges and universities are following:

Associate Arts/Associate Science Degree (AA/AS)

This is a two-year college degree. It is often awarded at community colleges, as well as many distance-learning programs. There are many different versions of this degree, which signify the area of study. For example, an AAS is an Associate Degree in Applied Science and an AFA is an Associate Degree in Fine Arts.

Examples of jobs which require at least an Associate Degree:

- Physical therapy assistant
- Dental assistant
- Radiation therapist
- Registered nurse
- Legal secretary

Professional Certificate

Although not officially considered a "degree," a professional certificate can be earned at community colleges and trade/technical schools. There are also many certificates for particular technologies, such as web developer or repair technician. These kinds of certificates can be completed relatively quickly and typically take from six weeks to two years to complete.

Examples of jobs requiring a professional certificate:

- Paralegal
- Hairstylist
- Interior decorator
- Nail technician
- Personal trainer
- Welder
- Chef
- Contractor

Bachelor of Arts/Bachelor of Science Degree (BA/BS)

A bachelor's degree (also called an undergraduate degree) is the standard term for a four-year college degree. Bachelor degree programs are offered in hundreds of subjects at four-year public and private colleges and universities. A bachelor's degree is a prerequisite for all graduate programs, meaning that a student must earn a bachelor's degree before applying to graduate school. Typically, during the first two years of a bachelor's degree program, students complete undergraduate general education courses. During the final two years, students complete the "upper division" courses in their major field of study.

Examples of jobs that require a Bachelor's Degree

- Graphic designer
- Financial analyst
- Software/civil/mechanical engineer
- Accountant
- Journalist

Graduate School Degrees

About 3 million new students enrolled in graduate school in 2015 (Source: http://nces. ed.gov/programs/coe). Graduate school is an advanced program of study focused on a particular academic discipline or profession, and requires students to submit an application and transcripts from their bachelor's degree program. In addition, most graduate schools require an aptitude test for the specific area of study. Depending on the field of study, admission into graduate school can be very competitive. Once admitted, students normally complete one to three years of courses to earn their graduate degree.

GRADUATE SCHOOL COMPARED TO UNDERGRADUATE EDUCATION

Compared to undergraduate courses, graduate school is a more concentrated course of study. The expectations regarding the quality and quantity of a student's academic work are greater. Graduate programs generally entail:

- Focused studies in a specific discipline with fewer elective possibilities
- Rigorous evaluation of student work by professors and peers
- Smaller classes with intensive student interaction
- Work experience via internships, teaching, or research
- Production of original research is often required

Types of Degrees Granted in Graduate School

Master of Arts/Master of Science Degree (MA/MS)—The master's degree requires at least a bachelor's degree as a prerequisite, and most programs require students to pass the GRE, the Graduate Record Exam. The master's degree is the most common graduate degree. It usually consists of a full-time, two-year program of study, but both part-time and accelerated programs are available. Master's degree programs can take as little as nine months or as much as four years, depending on the program and level of study.

Examples of jobs that require a Master's Degree:

- High school counselor
- Community college instructor
- Social worker
- Marriage, family, and child counselor
- Nurse practitioner

Doctorate of Philosophy (PhD)—A PhD is a doctoral degree, not a medical degree. This degree is specifically called a "doctor of philosophy" degree. The name can be misleading, because PhD degree holders are not necessarily philosophers (unless they earned their degree in philosophy!). The PhD degree is awarded in hundreds of fields of study. Typically, this degree requires several years of study beyond the master's degree. The number of years of study varies by discipline and by student. Some students complete their PhD degree in four years, and others take up to eight or more years of study depending on the field, the student's research topic, and the student's academic skills.

Examples of jobs that require a Doctorate:

- Clinical researcher
- Clinical psychologist
- University professor
- Astronomer
- Anthropologist

Professional School Degrees

A professional school is a distinct graduate school affiliated with the University of California and private four-year universities in California. Professional schools prepare students for careers in highly specialized fields of study. Only students who have earned at least a bachelor's degree and have taken the required entrance exam may apply to a professional school. The number of years it takes students to complete a professional degree varies by discipline and by student, but generally the degrees takes three to eight years to complete.

A few examples of professional school degrees include:

Doctor of Jurisprudence (JD/Law), Law School—This is the degree received by students following completion of a three-year course of study in law school. Along with the bar exams offered by individual states, it is the credential possessed by most practicing lawyers in this state.

Doctor of Medicine (MD/Medical), Medical School—This is the standard degree held by all physicians. An "MD" typically requires four years of graduate level coursework. After the degree is obtained, practicing doctors must then complete an internship and residency, each offering hands-on medical training at a working hospital. These latter two phases can take anywhere from three to eight years or more, depending on the doctor's choice of specialty.

Doctor of Veterinary Medicine (DVM), Veterinary School—To be accepted into a DVM program, a student must have documented experience working with animals, as well as a minimum of sixty college-level credit hours. Students in a DVM program are required to take courses such as animal pharmacology, animal pathology, diagnostic radiology, epidemiology, and equine care. The program includes coursework and clinical experiences, and often includes working in an animal veterinary hospital.

GRADUATION TIME BY DEGREE AND TYPE OF COLLEGE/UNIVERSITY

As a parent, you want to know how many years it will take your child to complete her desired degree. This is an important question for several reasons we have mentioned previously. The following table outlines the "typical" time to degree by type of college/degree. Keep in mind that some students may take longer, and a few students may even complete their degree in a shorter time period.

Degree	Colleges Where Offered	Typical Time to Graduate
Technical, trade, or vocational certificate	Community Colleges, Trade/technical schools	One to two years
Associate Degree	Community colleges	Two to three years
Bachelor's Degree	Four-year colleges and universities	Four to five years
Master's Degree	Four-year colleges and universities	Bachelor's degree + one to two years of additional study
Doctorate/Professional	Four-year colleges and universities	Bachelor's degree + Master's degree + two to three years of additional study + experience

Table 10   Typical Time to a College Degree

Chapter 7

Higher Education Options in California

"Success is where preparation and opportunity meet"
—Bobby Unser, Champion Race Car Driver

In the previous chapters, you learned how to help your child discover his unique interests and strengths, helped him determine which major areas of study align with his interests, and researched the numerous colleges that offer that major area of study. Now it is time to learn about the wide range of higher education options that will be available to your child upon his graduation from high school.

THE HIGHER EDUCATION MASTER PLAN IN CALIFORNIA

The public higher education system in the state of California is a three-tiered system designed to serve the educational needs of all students in the state. In 1960, the California legislature adopted landmark legislation which, for the first time in California history, established a commitment to guarantee that there would be a place in college for every California high school graduate or person otherwise qualified. This broad and extensive Master Plan governs higher education in California to this very day. The Master Plan clearly identifies three separate and distinct segments of California's higher education system and outlines the following important differences among the state's three public postsecondary education segments.

The University of California (UC)

The University of California is designated as the state's primary academic research institution and is charged by the state with providing undergraduate, graduate, and professional education. The state gives the UC system exclusive jurisdiction in public higher education for awarding doctoral degrees (with some exceptions—see CSU on the following page) and for instruction in law, medicine, dentistry, and veterinary medicine.

The California State University (CSU)

The California State University is designed to provide undergraduate education and graduate education through the master's degree level, including professional and teacher education. Faculty research is consistent with this primary function of instruction. Legislation passed in 2006 authorized the CSU system to award specific Doctorate of Education (EdD) degrees in educational leadership. Other doctorates can be awarded jointly with UC or an independent/private institution.

California Community Colleges

The California community college system is designated to provide academic and vocational instruction for students through the first two years of an undergraduate education. In addition to this primary mission, the community colleges are designed to provide remedial instruction, English as a Second Language courses, adult instruction, community service courses, economic workforce training services, and classes for lifelong learners.

Private Colleges and Universities

Although they are not addressed in California's Master Plan for Higher Education because they do not receive public tax revenue, California's private colleges and universities are an excellent choice for many students. There are seventy-six private, non-profit colleges and universities in the state. Unlike the University of California or the California State University systems, each California private college and university has its own governing board and its own admissions and enrollment policies. This independence allows for a diverse set of college opportunities for students in California.

Technical/Trade Schools

Technical and trade schools are privately run and also are not supported by state tax revenue. However, these schools can be an excellent choice for students who want their education to focus on job skill training. Most technical/trade schools focus on a particular set of skills that are taught to students looking to enter a specific career field. These are important schools that help to train workers to perform the tasks needed to work in critical fields, and they usually provide the education and training in a shorter period of time than traditional universities.

POLICIES FOR ADMISSION AND ENROLLMENT IN PUBLIC HIGHER EDUCATION SYSTEMS IN CALIFORNIA

The California Master Plan established the following policies for student admissions and enrollment were established with the goal of universal access and choice for all students in California:

- UC was to select from among the top one-eighth (12.5 percent) of the high school graduating class.*

- CSU was to select from among the top one-third (33.3 percent) of the high school graduating class.*

- California community colleges were to admit any student capable of benefiting from higher education.

    *UC/CSU Admissions Guarantee: In a subsequent legislation modification, the Master Plan now provides that all California students in the top one-eighth (UC) or top one-third (CSU) of the statewide high school graduating class are guaranteed a place somewhere in the UC or CSU system. Students must apply on time and, although they are guaranteed a place somewhere in the UC or CSU system, the place will not necessarily be at their first choice campus or in their first choice major.

In this chapter, we will provide extensive details regarding the college choices available to your child, as well as the cost to attend, and the locations of each campus.

CALIFORNIA COMMUNITY COLLEGE SYSTEM

The California community college system is composed of 112 two-year public institutions. In 2013, more than 2.6 million students were enrolled in community colleges in California, making it the largest system of higher education in the nation.

A California resident may attend any community college campus in the state. Students may complete the first two years of their four-year education at a community college, and if they meet specific requirements, they then can transfer to a CSU, a UC, or a private four-year college to complete their Bachelor's degree.

2 years of Community College

+

2 Years at a Four-Year University or College

=

Bachelors of Arts/Science Degree

If they are not interested in transferring, community college students can also choose to enroll in an associate (two-year) degree or a professional certificate program in a wide range of occupational fields. These fields include health occupations, electronics and computer sciences, business and finance, agriculture, police and fire science, food science, building and landscaping trades, technical and industrial trades, and many others. Community colleges have up-to-date equipment and facilities and vocational instructors who are experts in their fields. Depending on the occupation your child selects, training may take from six months to two years.

Parents are often surprised to learn that several community colleges within the state offer on-campus housing or dormitories. Therefore, your child is not limited to only attending the community college closest to home.

CALIFORNIA COMMUNITY COLLEGE CAMPUS LOCATIONS

Locations of all of California's community college campuses can be found on the California Community College Chancellor's Office website. Searches can be performed by region (twelve regions in the state), as well as alphabetically or by academic program.

To locate a specific campus, go to: http://californiacommunitycolleges.cccco.edu/maps/map.asp.

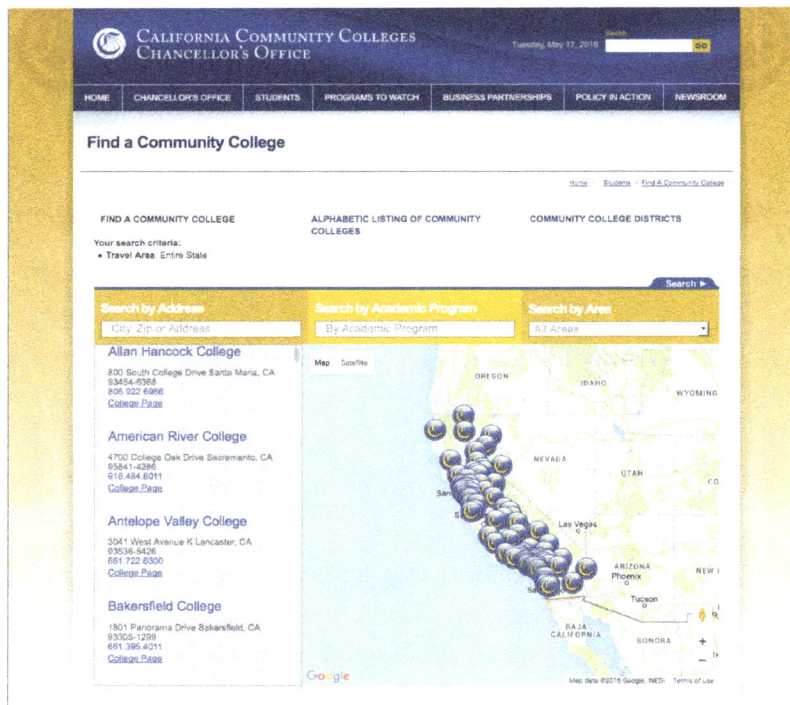

Figure 14   California Community College System Website

Cost to Attend a Community College

An enrollment fee is charged to every student who takes courses for credit. In 2015, the fee charged to state residents was $46 per unit. Therefore, a full-time student enrolled for 12 units each semester could expect to pay $552 per semester, or $1,108 annually in enrollment fees. Other fees are often charged as well, including campus activity fees, health center fees, and parking fees, but these are normally very minimal.

Financial aid available includes: fee waivers, grants, scholarships, work-study programs, and loans. This money can be used to help pay for fees, books, supplies, and, in some cases, living expenses. Students who enroll full-time generally receive more financial aid than part-time students. (Financial aid will be covered in more detail in Chapter 10.)

CALIFORNIA STATE UNIVERSITY (CSU)

With 23 campuses, 447,000 students, and 45,000 faculty and staff, the California State University system is one of the largest university systems in the entire country. The CSU system is often the gateway institution for thousands of students seeking a bachelor's degree in California, and especially for those who seek professional training as teachers, nurses, social workers, and engineers.

Academic excellence has been achieved by the California State University through a distinguished faculty, whose primary responsibility is superior teaching.

The CSU system offers more than 1,800 bachelor's and master's degree programs in 357 subject areas. Many programs are offered so that students can complete upper-division and graduate requirements through part-time, late afternoon and/or evening courses. In addition, a variety of teaching and school service credential programs are available. A limited number of doctoral degrees are offered jointly with the University of California and with private institutions in California. In 2006, the CSU system was authorized to independently offer Doctor of Education (EdD) degree programs for educational administrators.

Descriptions of each CSU campus can be found on the website of www.csumentor.edu.

On this site you will find such valuable features as:

- Comparative View—Comparison of the 23 CSU campus statistics with sorting options.
- Campus Facts—Detailed campus profiles with photos, links, and videos.
- Distance Search—Find the campus closest to any zip code.
- FAQs—University Selection—Frequently asked questions and answers about specific CSU campuses.
- Inquire to the CSU Campuses—Find a direct way to contact the campus for more information.
- Explore Majors/Search CSU Degrees—Find majors or degrees by CSU campus or key-words.

Estimated Average 2015–2016 CSU Academic Year Expenses			
	Commuting from home	Living in campus housing	Living away from home/off-campus
Tuition Fee	$5,472	$5,472	$5,472
Miscellaneous Fees	1,226	1,226	1,226
Books and Supplies	1,719	1,719	1,719
Meals and Housing	4,532	12,080	12,089
Transportation	1,345	1,169	1,391
Miscellaneous Personal	1,364	1,364	1,364
TOTAL	$15,658	$23,030	$23,261

Table 11   Annual Cost to Attend a CSU Campus. Source: https://secure.csumentor.edu/faq/finaid_costs.asp

CSU Campus Locations

The twenty-three CSU campus locations are shown in the following figure.

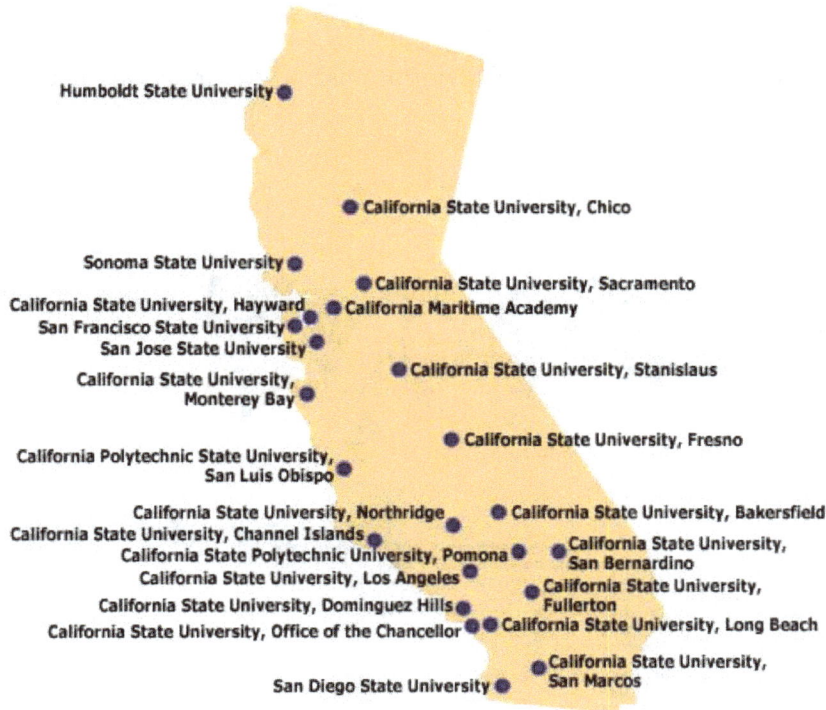

Figure 15   California State University Campus Locations

THE UNIVERSITY OF CALIFORNIA (UC) SYSTEM

The University of California system offers students world-class educational and research opportunities and generates a wide range of benefits that touch the lives of millions throughout the world. The UC system encompasses more than 200,000 students, 120,000 faculty and staff, and more than 1.3 million alumni. The University of California is also actively involved in locations beyond its main campuses in national laboratories, medical centers, and communities throughout California, around the world, and online. The University of California includes nine undergraduate campuses—Berkeley, Davis, Irvine, Los Angeles, Merced, Riverside, San Diego, Santa Barbara, and Santa Cruz. A tenth campus, UC San Francisco, offers professional and graduate programs in the health sciences. UC has built an international reputation for academic excellence, with undergraduate education as one of its highest priorities. UC has outstanding academic programs, faculty, libraries, and research facilities. Whether your child wants a broad liberal arts education, preparation for graduate study, or training for a particular profession, UC has a program to meet his needs.

UC graduates enjoy high acceptance rates at graduate and professional schools and compete successfully in the job market with graduates of other top universities and colleges. Many of UC's graduates become leaders in their fields.

For additional information on each UC campus, visit www. universityofcalifornia.edu.

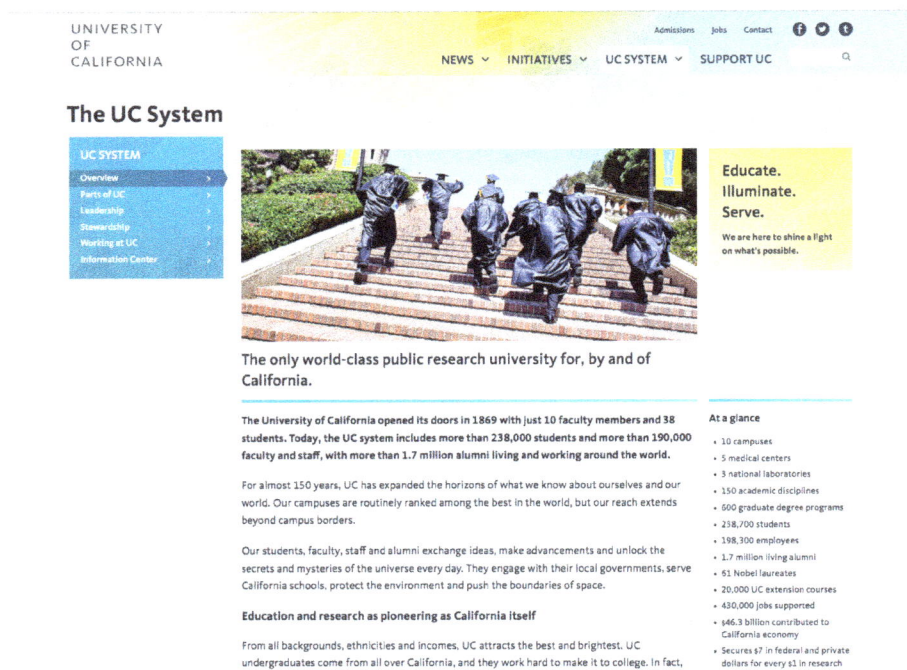

Figure 16   University of California System Website

Estimated Average 2015–2016 UC Academic Year Expenses	Living on campus	Living off campus
Tuition and fees	$13,300	$13,300
Books and supplies	$1,500	$1,500
Health insurance allowance/fee	$1,900	$1,900
Room and board	$14,000	$9,300
Personal/transportation	$2,400	$3,200
TOTAL	$33,100	$29,200

Table 12   Annual Cost to Attend a University of California Campus—California Resident. Source: http://admission.universityofcalifornia.edu/paying-for-uc/tuition-and-cost/

UC Campus Locations

Figure 17   University of California Campus Locations

INDEPENDENT/PRIVATE COLLEGES AND UNIVERSITIES IN CALIFORNIA

Most private colleges and universities in California are members of the Association of Independent California Colleges and Universities. AICCU represents seventy-six (76) private, nonprofit colleges and universities in California. The core mission of AICCU members is to improve lives through higher education. AICCU colleges are committed to the public good and are incredibly diverse—ranging from large to small traditional liberal arts colleges to nationally ranked research universities. Private colleges offer faith-based, "nontraditional" programs of study; as well as professional schools that specialize in business, law, medicine, and more. Accreditation by the Western Association of Schools and Colleges (WASC) is required for membership, as is fulfilling a public purpose through nonprofit status.

The state's independent colleges and universities provide creative and intellectual higher education resources to assure California's future economic vitality. AICCU colleges and universities offer programs at more than 100 locations across California, contributing to the betterment of the state in many ways, especially through providing access to a quality higher education for California's diverse population.

AICCU Campus Locations

Detailed information on and the location of each of the AICCU private colleges/universities located in the state can be found online at: http://www.aiccu.edu/member-colleges.

Estimated Cost to Attend AICCU Private Universities and Colleges—2015–16 Academic Year

	California Private/ Independent Colleges
Registration Fees and Tuition	$24,300 to $46,952
Books and Supplies	$1,826
Room and Board	$7,650 to $13,970
Transportation	$1,496
Personal Expenses	$1,364
Total Estimated Yearly Cost	$41,100 to $65,608

Table 13   California Private/Independent College Costs for 2015–2016

TECHNICAL/TRADE SCHOOLS

Technical/trade schools typically focus on job skill training. Most schools focus on a particular set of skills that are taught to students looking to enter a specific career field. These schools train workers to perform the tasks needed to work in critical fields, and they usually provide the education and training in a shorter period of time than traditional universities.

A technical/trade school might be just the right fit for your child if he knows exactly what he wants to do when he graduates from high school. These schools are great options for hands-on learners who have difficulty learning in a traditional classroom setting.

If you think that a trade school is right for your child, set aside ample time to research all of the possible schools, and especially research the accreditation and reputation of the school.

Average Cost to Attend Technical/Trade Schools in California (Sample)

Name of Trade	Costs of Schooling	Length of Program	Degree Level	Job Type	Mean Annual Wage
Accounting	$3,000–$10,000	6 Months to 2 Years	Certification or AA	Accountant	$72,500
Culinary	$17,500–$47,000	6 Months to 2 Years	Certificate or Higher	Chef	$45,000
Nursing	$5,000–$40,000	1 to 2 Years	Certificate or Higher	LPN & RN	$48,500–$65,470
Welding	$4,000–$15,000	3 Months to 2 Years	Certificate or Higher	Welder	$36,300
Automotive	$1,000–$20,000	6 Months to 2 Years	Certificate or Higher	Auto Service Tech	$42,500

http://www.uncollege.org/vocational-schools-a-great-alternative/ http://www.howmuchisit.org/

Technical/Trade School Campus Locations

To research the type and location of every trade school in California, a helpful website is: http://www.trade-schools.net/locations/california-schools-directory.asp.

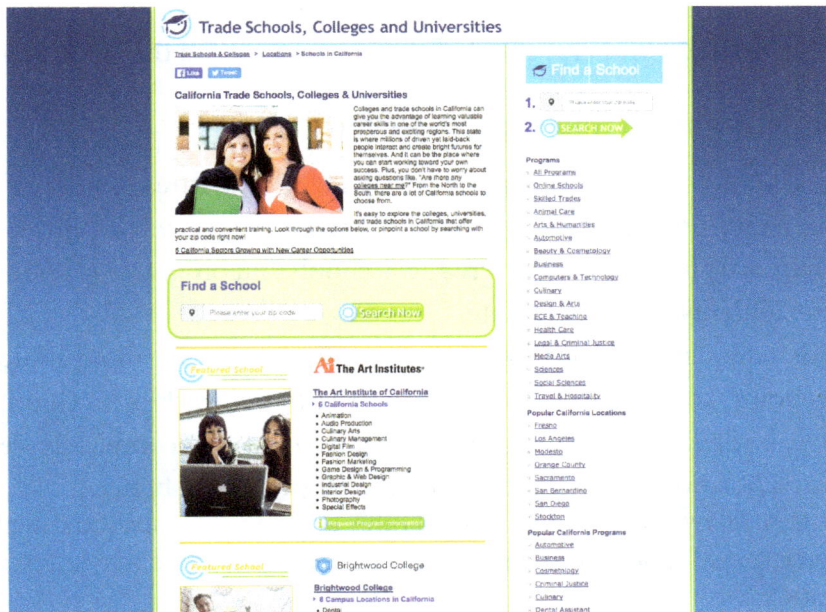

Figure 18   Directory of Trade Schools in California

What Every Good Trade School Must Have on Its Record

Be sure to keep the following necessities in mind to make sure your child will receive top quality at a trade school: http://www.business.com/education/trade-schools.

A Trade School Must Be Accredited

Accreditation guarantees that your child will be receiving a quality education. Unfortunately, there are some trade schools out there which claim to be something that they are not. If a school is accredited or meets learning standards set out by an accrediting agency, your child's education will be taken seriously by future employers.

A Trade School Must Have a Good Industry Reputation

Do not spend your time and money on a school with a bad reputation. Ask around about the reputation of the trade school at places of employment in this field, and see if they have hired any graduates from this school. In addition, ask the trade school if it works closely with employers in the community. Good trade schools will do this through job fairs and seminars, and will often use professional tradesmen and women to teach courses.

A Trade School Must Offer Hands-On Instruction with Up-to-Date Materials

Your child is not going to a trade school to sit in a classroom and learn about what he will be doing once the program is over. A trade school is about hands-on training to get a feel for the profession before he begins looking for a job. Take some time out to visit the school and make sure that students are immersed in their future career using the latest tools.

A Trade School Must Have a Good Retention Rate

Every trade school does have a retention rate, whether it desires to publish it or not. Ask the school about its retention rate to make sure that the students who do enroll *actually finish* the program. There are plenty of good, accredited schools and programs to choose from, so do not pick one that students do not complete.

Overall, trade schools are becoming more and more popular for those students who want to "get in and get out," knowing exactly what to expect in the workforce. Good trade schools can be expensive, but affordable options are available. The price completely depends on the school you choose; however, more expensive doesn't always mean better.

Please note that many community colleges offer comparable vocational/technical certificates to those programs found at trade schools, and these programs may offer a more affordable training option for your student.

Chapter 8

Freshman Admission

Look at a day when you are supremely satisfied at the end.
It's not a day when you lounge around doing nothing;
it's a day you've had everything to do and you've done it
—Margaret Thatcher

What is a freshman? If your child is planning to enroll in college directly after her senior year in high school, she will be applying to enroll as a "freshman." (We will cover transfer admission requirements in Chapter 9.)

As we covered in Chapter 7, a huge benefit of being a resident of California is the abundance of higher education options available for your child. As you research the options available, keep in mind that admission policies at colleges and universities throughout the state vary widely. For example, there are only a few admissions criteria for the community college system, while freshman admissions requirements for both public and private four-year institutions are much more demanding and complex.

Individual colleges and universities differ widely in how they evaluate admissions application information. One college, for example, may place a great deal of importance on grades and test scores, while another college may focus more on factors such as special talents and skills. In this chapter we will cover the admissions criteria and essential factors that each higher education system in California uses to make freshman admissions decisions.

CALIFORNIA COMMUNITY COLLEGE FRESHMAN ADMISSION

Admission as a freshman to any one of California's 112 community colleges is quite simple. Your child will be admitted to the community college of her choice if she meets at least one of the following conditions:

- 18 years of age or older
- A high school graduate or possesses the equivalent of a high school diploma (GED)
- California resident

APPLYING FOR ADMISSION

Applying to a California community college is very easy. There are two ways to apply: online or on paper. Online applications for most of the California community colleges can be found at www.cccapply.org or through each college's individual website.

All California citizens are eligible to apply to any of the 112 community colleges located throughout the state.

The steps to applying and enrolling in community college may vary a little, but in general include the following steps for first-time students:

1. Submit admissions application to the community college.
2. Complete college assessment testing for correct course placement.
3. Submit application for financial aid. Submit high school transcripts.
4. Complete new student orientation.
5. Schedule an appointment with a counselor to discuss appropriate classes for the first semester.
6. Register for classes.

While California community colleges enroll students year-round, your child should still apply as early as possible.

ASSESSMENT TESTING FOR COMMUNITY COLLEGE COURSE PLACEMENT

Most community colleges do not require standardized test scores like the ACT or SAT for admissions. However, community colleges do require some type of placement tests to determine what level of math and English courses your child will need to enroll in for her first year. Certain scores on the SAT, ACT, or Smarter Balanced tests she took in high school may exempt your child from these placement tests. Standardized test scores may be required for admissions if your child wants to enroll in a selective program at a community college, such as nursing, computer science, or law enforcement.

Community College Placement Tests—COMPASS and ACCUPLACER

The ACT Compass and College Board ACCUPLACER are placement tests offered at the community college level to determine student placement into the correct levels of reading, writing, and math courses. Which test is utilized (Compass or ACCUPLACER) depends on the specific college. The format is multiple choice, administered on a computer, and administered throughout the academic year on each of the community college campuses. The higher a student scores on the Compass or ACCUPLACER test, the higher level of reading, writing, and/or math course she will be able to take at the college. This translates into fewer remedial classes your child will need to take (and pay for) to "catch up." Some Community Colleges have begun using multiple measures for the assessment process, so it is always good to check with your local college regarding recent assessment measures.

CALIFORNIA STATE UNIVERSITY (CSU) FRESHMAN ADMISSIONS

As discussed in Chapter 7, there are twenty-three CSU campuses throughout the state. The admissions requirements for the CSU system are outlined below.

Freshman Admission Requirements for California Residents

CSU admissions offices use the following three factors to determine student eligibility. Most applicants who are admitted to the CSU system meet or exceed the standards in each of the following areas:

1. Specific high school courses completed (referred to as the "A-G" courses)

The most important factor in CSU admissions is the completion of the A-G coursework as outlined in the following list. The CSU requires this minimum 15-unit pattern of high school course completion for admission for all first-time freshmen. Each unit is equal to a year of study in a subject area. A grade of C or better is required for each course.

"A-G" Requirements

- History/social science ("a")—Two years, including one year of world history, cultures and historical geography, and one year of U.S. history, or one-half year of U.S. history and one-half year of American government or civics.

- English ("b")—Four years of college preparatory English that includes frequent and regular writing, reading of classic and modern literature, and practice listening and speaking.

- Mathematics ("c")—Three years of college-preparatory mathematics that include the topics covered in elementary and advanced algebra and two- and three-dimensional geometry.

- Laboratory science ("d")—Two years of laboratory science including at least one year of biology and one year of physical science.

- Language other than English ("e")—Two years of the same language other than English or equivalent to the second-level of high school instruction. American Sign Language is acceptable.

- Visual and performing arts ("f")—One year, including dance, drama/theater, music, or visual art.

- College-preparatory elective ("g")—One year chosen from the "a-g" courses beyond those used to satisfy the requirements above, or courses that have been approved solely for use as "g" electives.

2. Grades in "A-G" Courses

The grades your child earns in her high school A-G courses are the second most important factor in CSU admission decisions. It is very important to note that high school grade point averages (GPAs) will be calculated based on your child's earned grades in all "A-G" classes completed *after the 9th grade year*.

3. SAT/ACT Test Scores

The third important factor in CSU admissions are standardized test scores. The SAT and/or ACT test scores are required by all CSU campuses UNLESS your child has a GPA above 3.0. The CSU uses a calculation called an "eligibility index" that combines your child's high school GPA with the score she earns on either the SAT or ACT. Even if your child has a GPA above 3.0, it is still useful for her to take either the SAT or ACT, as the score may indicate if she does not need to take the required English and math placement tests before enrolling at the CSU.

Chapter 8

Freshman Admission

Look at a day when you are supremely satisfied at the end.
It's not a day when you lounge around doing nothing;
it's a day you've had everything to do and you've done it
—Margaret Thatcher

What is a freshman? If your child is planning to enroll in college directly after her senior year in high school, she will be applying to enroll as a "freshman." (We will cover transfer admission requirements in Chapter 9.)

As we covered in Chapter 7, a huge benefit of being a resident of California is the abundance of higher education options available for your child. As you research the options available, keep in mind that admission policies at colleges and universities throughout the state vary widely. For example, there are only a few admissions criteria for the community college system, while freshman admissions requirements for both public and private four-year institutions are much more demanding and complex.

Individual colleges and universities differ widely in how they evaluate admissions application information. One college, for example, may place a great deal of importance on grades and test scores, while another college may focus more on factors such as special talents and skills. In this chapter we will cover the admissions criteria and essential factors that each higher education system in California uses to make freshman admissions decisions.

Encourage your child to be competitive in the application process by applying early, answering all of the questions in the application, and staying current with all of the deadlines set by each campus to which she applies.

The online CSU admissions application is located on the CSU Mentor website at www. csumentor.edu and is available 24 hours a day, 7 days a week. Have your child start her online application in late summer to early fall of her senior year. One advantage to applying online is that she does not have to complete the entire application at one time—whatever information is entered can be saved and the application completed over time.

APPLYING TO MORE THAN ONE CSU CAMPUS

Each CSU campus independently processes and makes admission decisions for all applicants. If your child has an interest in more than one CSU campus, she will need to apply separately to each campus. The online application automatically fills in most information for each additional CSU admission application, which saves some time and work. Your child will then only need to complete the campus-specific information, verify her information, upload the application fee, and then submit the final application to each campus.

CSUs—COST TO APPLY

Each admission application your child files requires a $55 nonrefundable application fee, which may not be transferred to another term.

Fee Waiver Eligibility

In the case of financial hardship, all CSU campuses allow a limited number of application fee waivers for residents of California. If your child files the admission application via CSU Mentor, the fee waiver request is included in the online system as part of the application process. Your child will be notified at the time she applies online if she qualifies for the fee waiver. In situations where the online application is unable to determine eligibility for a fee waiver, your child will need to submit the request for an application fee waiver directly to the campus admission office(s). The campus will inform your child directly if she does not end up qualifying for the fee waiver. Only California residents are eligible and may use up to a maximum of four admissions application fee waivers.

The Educational Opportunity Program Application

The Educational Opportunity Program (EOP) is designed to improve the retention rates of historically low-income and educationally disadvantaged students. Students who have the potential and demonstrated motivation to perform satisfactorily at a CSU, but may have not been able to realize their potential because of their economic or educational background, may qualify for this program. The program provides admission and academic assistance to EOP-eligible undergraduate students. In many cases, the program also offers financial assistance to eligible students.

Each CSU campus (except the California Maritime Academy) has an EOP program for low-income students who are California residents and are disadvantaged because of their economic and educational backgrounds. Students with a history of low income who need academic and financial assistance may apply for the program. EOP accepts students who do not meet regular admission criteria, as well as those who qualify for regular admission. Be sure to indicate on the undergraduate application for admission if your child is applying through EOP. The EOP application is separate from the regular CSU admissions application, requires more information than the regular application, and has the same November 30 deadline. The link for the EOP application can be found at: https://secure.csumentor.edu/admissionapp/eop_apply.asp.

UNIVERSITY OF CALIFORNIA FRESHMAN ADMISSIONS

The admission guidelines at the University of California are designed to ensure your child is well-prepared to compete, succeed, and complete her education at the University of California.

If your child is interested in applying to the University of California as a freshman, she must satisfy the following minimum requirements:

- Complete a minimum of 15 college-preparatory A-G courses with at least 11 of them completed prior to the beginning of her senior year.

- Earn a grade point average (GPA) of 3.0 or better in the completed A–G courses with no grade earned lower than a C. GPA for admissions is calculated using her 10th and 11th A–G coursework only.

- Meet the examination requirement by taking the ACT Plus Writing or the SAT Reasoning Test by December of her senior year. Although UC does not require SAT Subject Tests, certain campuses still strongly recommend them.

- Provide personal statement responses designed to tell UC admissions officers about her hopes, ambitions, life experiences, and inspirations.

- Provide a detailed list of her extracurricular activities, volunteer experience, work experience, awards, special talents, leadership experience, and activities outside of the school environment.

Most four-year colleges and universities look at the high school profile of each applicant. A school profile is a one- or two-page document that includes pertinent information about the school and the community. School profiles usually include information on the size of the high school, the percentage of students who go on to college, the average ACT and SAT scores of the previous graduating class(es), and information on how GPA is calculated. While the transcript provides admissions officers with information about the student, the school profile provides information about the high school the student is attending.

UC Admissions Selection Criteria

UC admissions officers spend a great deal of time evaluating your child's academic achievements in light of the opportunities available to her and her demonstrated capacity to contribute to the intellectual life at UC. For the Fall 2017 admissions, the comprehensive admissions review includes:

1. Academic grade point average in all completed "a-g" courses, including additional points for completed UC-certified honors courses.

2. Scores on the following tests: ACT Plus Writing or the SAT Reasoning Test.

3. Number of, content of, and performance in academic courses beyond the minimum "a-g" requirements.

4. Number of and performance in UC-approved honors, Advanced Placement, International Baccalaureate Higher Level, and transferable college courses.

5. Identification by UC as being ranked in the top 9 percent of the high school class at the end of your child's junior year (Eligible in the Local Context, or ELC).

6. Quality of your child's senior-year program as measured by the type and number of academic courses in progress or planned.

7. Quality of your child's academic performance relative to the educational opportunities available at her high school.

8. Outstanding academic performance in one or more specific subject areas.

9. Outstanding work in one or more special projects in any academic field of study.

10. Recent, marked improvement in academic performance as demonstrated by academic GPA and the quality of coursework completed or in progress.

11. Special talents, achievements, and awards in a particular field, such as visual and performing arts, communication or athletic endeavors. Special skills, such as demonstrated written and oral proficiency in other languages. Special interests, such as intensive study and exploration of other cultures. Special experiences that demonstrate unusual promise for leadership, such as significant community service or significant participation in student government or other significant experiences or achievements that demonstrate the student's promise for contributing to the intellectual vitality of a campus.

12. Completion of a special project undertaken in the context of your child's high school curriculum or in conjunction with special school events, projects, or programs.

13. Academic accomplishments in light of your child's life experiences and special circumstances, including but not limited to: disabilities, low family income, first generation to attend college, need to work, disadvantaged social or educational environment, difficult personal and family situations or circumstances, refugee status, or veteran status.

14. Geographical location of your child's secondary school and residence.

UC—HOW TO APPLY FOR FRESHMAN ADMISSION

UC opens the online application starting in early August and the filing period is from November 1 to 30 of each year. Encourage your child to apply early in her senior year, as UC campuses do not accept applications after November 30. Encourage your child to apply early, answering all of the questions in the application, and to stay current with all of the deadlines set by each campus to which she applies.

The UC application website can be found at: http://admission.universityofcalifornia.edu/how-to-apply/index.html.

The UC application website is available 24 hours a day, 7 days a week. Have your child start her online application in late summer to early fall. One advantage to starting the online application early is that she does not have to complete the entire application at one time—whatever information is entered can be saved and the application completed later.

ADMISSIONS APPLICATION FEES

The nonrefundable application fee is $70 for each UC campus to which your child applies. Your child must charge the application fee to a credit card or mark the box that she will submit the fee immediately via a check or money order.

ADMISSIONS APPLICATION FEE WAIVERS

UC will waive application fees for up to four campuses for qualified students (U.S. citizens and permanent residents) who meet the fee waiver requirements based on your family income and number of people in the family. Your child can apply for a fee waiver as part of the online application process and will immediately know whether she qualifies before submitting information regarding your family's income and the number of people supported by that income. Students who qualify for fee waivers and who choose to select more than four UC campuses must pay $70 for each additional campus.

IMPORTANT TIPS FOR THE UC APPLICANT

Only ONE Freshman Admission Application Is Needed for All NINE UC Campuses

Your child may apply to as many UC undergraduate campuses as she likes by completing just one online application. Each one of her selected campuses will receive her application.

Be Sure to Apply to More Than One UC Campus

Encourage your child to apply to more than one UC campus to significantly increase her chances of being admitted to a campus she wants to attend. All UC campuses—without exception—provide outstanding opportunities for her to learn and grow.

Report ALL Test Results

Freshmen applicants must take the ACT with Writing or SAT Reasoning Test and order score reports from the testing agency no later than December of their senior year. The official test results must arrive to the UC campus by January 15th. Your child can have a report sent to just one campus and the report will be shared with all the campuses to which she ends up applying. Be sure to emphasize to your child that she must take the writing portion of the SAT or the ACT because the UC system uses the scores to meet UC eligibility, and her scores can be used for course placement during her freshman year in college.

File on Time

UC admission applications must be submitted online between November 1 and November 30. UC campuses do not accept applications after that date.

Answering the UC Personal Insight Questions

- Freshmen must select 4 questions to respond to from the 8 options.
- Each response has a limit of 350 words.
- All questions have equal value; there is no advantage or disadvantage to choosing certain questions over others.
- Students **cannot** respond to more than 4 questions in total.

Additional Comments Section Instructions from the UC application:

If there's anything else you want us to know about you, now's your chance. This shouldn't be an essay, but rather a place to explain unusual personal or family circumstances, or anything that may be unclear in other parts of the application.

This section should not be used to answer an additional personal insight question.

What Are the Freshmen Questions?

1. Describe an example of your leadership experience in which you have positively influenced others, helped resolve disputes, or contributed to group efforts over time.
2. Every person has a creative side, and it can be expressed in many ways: problem solving, original and innovative thinking, and artistically, to name a few. Describe how you express your creative side.
3. What would you say is your greatest talent or skill? How have you developed and demonstrated that talent over time?
4. Describe how you have taken advantage of a significant educational opportunity or worked to overcome an educational barrier you have faced.

5. Describe the most significant challenge you have faced and the steps you have taken to overcome this challenge. How has this challenge affected your academic achievement?

6. Describe your favorite academic subject and explain how it has influenced you.

7. What have you done to make your school or your community a better place?

8. What is the one thing that you think sets you apart from other candidates applying to the University of California?

Tips on Answering the Personal Insight Questions

Start Early

- Encourage your child to start writing her draft answers early, allowing time for reflection, thoughtful preparation, and revision.

- Suggest that she not *overly* focus on style or structure. Admissions does not grade on style—creativity, entertainment, or uniqueness—UC admissions places value on content.

- Does she make herself the focal point? Is she using "I" and "my" statements?

- Is she providing new information in a response? Is she repeating herself or adding depth or clarity to her application?

- Remind her that the personal insight responses are NOT reviewed in a vacuum. The freshmen review process is comprehensive.

Use a Computer or Laptop to Compose the Personal Statement

Encourage your child to use a word processing program to be able to edit, spell check, and save her responses. She may then import her answers into the online application.

Write Persuasively

Review your child's responses to ensure that she presents her information and ideas in a focused, deliberate, and meaningful manner. Encourage your child to offer specific and concrete examples to support her points, and focus on herself, not other people. A personal response to a question that is simply a list of qualities or accomplishments is usually not persuasive.

Proofread

In addition to checking her spelling, ensure that your child proofreads her work to check to see that grammar is correct and that the statement flows smoothly.

Solicit Feedback

Your child's personal insight responses should reflect her own ideas and be written by her alone, even though others—such as family, teachers, and friends—can offer valuable suggestions.

Have your child ask for advice from whomever she wants, but do not allow her to plagiarize from sources or use anyone's published words but her own.

Copy and Paste

Once your child is satisfied with her responses, make sure she saves the document in plain text and pastes it into the space provided in the online application. Ensure that she proofreads the statements one more time to make sure no odd characters or line breaks have appeared during the cut-and-paste process.

Relax

This is just one of many pieces of information that admissions offices consider in reviewing applications. It is very important to remind your child that the admissions decision *will not* be based solely on her personal insight responses.

Resource Links

The following sites have further information regarding the freshman admissions process for the UC system:

Freshman questions & directions

http://admission.universityofcalifornia.edu/how-to-apply/personal-questions/freshman/index.html

Guide for freshman applicants (brainstorming worksheet)

http://admission.universityofcalifornia.edu/how-to-apply/files/uc-personal-questions-guide-freshman.pdf

Writing tips

http://admission.universityofcalifornia.edu/how-to-apply/personal-questions/writing-tips/index.html

Video

http://admission.universityofcalifornia.edu/how-to-apply/personal-questions/index.html

FAQs about the personal insight questions

http://admission.universityofcalifornia.edu/counselors/q-and-a/personal-questions/index.html

PRIVATE COLLEGE/UNIVERSITY FRESHMAN ADMISSIONS

California's nonprofit, independent colleges and universities are often referred to as "private colleges." These universities are not supported by state taxes, unlike the University of California, California State University, or California community college systems.

California is home to seventy-six nonprofit private colleges and universities. These types of colleges focus on the individual student and, because each college and university is unique, their admission requirements vary. Applicants for private college admission are evaluated on past achievement, future promise, and "fit" with the college's mission and goals. All applicants are treated as individuals and are personally evaluated by an admissions officer.

Generally, admission requirements at private colleges and universities fall into four categories: (1) admission requirements similar to the University of California; (2) admission requirements similar to the California State University system; (3) admission requirements that accept only the top ten percent of students; and (4) very specific admission requirements—in addition to a well-rounded curriculum—related to the college's specialty, for example, experience in the visual or performing arts.

Applying to Private Colleges and Universities

The terms "private" and "independent" are used interchangeably to describe colleges and universities that are not supported by state funding, and therefore can be much more wide-ranging in their academic offerings, admissions policies, cost of attendance, and campus life. Although many students think that they will not be able to afford an education at a private college, often they receive financial aid packages that compare favorably with those from public colleges and universities.

Applying to a private college is usually more involved, however, than applying to a CSU or UC. Usually applicants need to write a personal essay, fill out a more complicated application form, get letters of recommendation from their high school counselors and teachers, and may need to include writing samples from class work. Private colleges have different deadlines for admissions applications and financial aid, so it is crucial to be well informed about each college's policies, and to complete applications in a timely manner. It is also an excellent idea to have visited the college before your child applies or once she has been accepted in order to help make a decision about whether to attend that college.

As noted in Chapter 7, the best website for researching private colleges and universities in California is www.aiccu.edu/. While doing research, be sure to have your child review each college's mission and vision statement to determine which ones might be a good fit.

After conducting initial research, your child should e-mail or call the colleges she is interested in and ask for an application packet. She can find addresses and phone numbers by looking through the college's online website. Most private colleges have online applications on their websites or PDF applications for students to download and print.

Application Tips

- Read the application packet as soon as your child receives it to make sure that she has taken the necessary SAT or ACT tests required for admission. Most colleges will accept either test, some require SAT subject tests, and most require students to take these tests by December of their senior year.

- Read the application carefully to find out what the application deadlines are, the topic for the personal essay, and other requirements such as writing samples, video, or audio tapes of performances or interviews.

- Find out if your child needs to obtain written recommendations from teachers and/or counselors.

- On the college's admissions website, look for a form entitled "Counselor Recommendation." Have your child fill out the top portion with her name, address, social security number, and any other information such as her senior class schedule, then sign it, and give it to her high school counselor or other school official to complete.

Your child should submit her application online, or mail a hard copy of the application directly to the college. If she sends any college documents through the U.S. Mail, be sure to make a copy and ask for a Certificate of Mailing. The Certificate of Mailing documents that an item was mailed out on time. Encourage your child to keep Certificate of Mailing receipts for test registrations, college and scholarship applications, and financial aid forms in a safe place.

TECHNICAL/TRADE SCHOOL ADMISSIONS

A technical/trade school is substantially easier to enter than a traditional college, and many students turn to a trade school to fulfill their need for a higher education program of study. It is very important that students choose a trade school that will prepare them for the job that they actually desire, since the entire curriculum will be based around this trade.

The advantage of a trade school is it can prepare students for a career in two years or less. Trade schools offer career-focused education that prepares students for success in diverse fields such as industrial technology, cosmetology, graphic design, medical billing, and culinary arts. A trade school may be a good postsecondary educational option if your child is interested in a shorter degree program than traditional colleges and universities offer.

Trade School Admission Requirements

Admission to any accredited trade school program requires your child to possess a high school diploma or its equivalent. Some programs require high school graduates to have earned a minimum 2.0 grade point average. Students applying with lower grades from high school may be able to gain full acceptance into the program after taking and passing remedial courses. Grade point average requirements usually do not apply to students who have earned a General Education Diploma (GED).

With a diploma in her possession, your child will need to fill out a trade school application. This application will ask questions about her, the specific trade programs that she is interested in, her educational background, the career goals she has set for herself, and her work history, if any.

Once the trade school application has been turned in, she will need to meet with an admissions counselor. This counselor will review the application with her to clarify her answers and ensure that she is enrolled in the right program, at the right level.

Standardized Placement Tests for Trade Schools

Completing one or more standardized placement tests is another requirement that students must meet to enter a trade school. The ACT Compass is an exam used by most trade schools as part of the admissions process. This test is intended to see whether an applicant has fundamental math, reading, and writing skills as determined by their test scores. A trade school may have a minimum score requirement for admission or use this score to determine which courses best meet the needs of an applicant. Other standardized placement tests that a trade school might use for enrollment may include the ACT and the SAT.

Be sure to set up a portal account for each individual school your child is applying to. Once an admissions application has been submitted through this portal, many schools will send all communication from that point forward through the school's portal system.

Chapter 9

Transfer Admission

"If you have the courage to begin, you have the courage to succeed"
—David Viscott, Author/Actor

A "transfer student" is primarily defined as a student who has completed college course work after high school, and has accumulated enough college credits to transfer to a four-year college or university.

During the 2015–2016 school year, more than 67,500 students transferred from a California community college to the University of California and California State University systems combined, and more than 20,000 students transferred from a California community college to California independent colleges (Source: https://secure.californiacolleges.edu/).

BENEFITS OF TRANSFERRING

A California community college is a great place to start if your child's ultimate goal is to obtain a bachelor's degree. Beginning the path to a four-year degree at a California community college has two major benefits: admission priority and cost savings.

ADMISSION PRIORITY

Transfer students from all California community colleges *have the highest* admissions priority of all students applying to the UC and CSU. In addition, several community colleges have transfer agreements with UC and CSU campuses to help students make a smooth transition. These formal admission agreements allow courses from both institutions to satisfy degree requirements. Furthermore, these agreements allow students to complete their first two years of college at the community college level and, in certain cases, be guaranteed admission to a four-year university to complete the last two years of their bachelor's degree program.

WHAT IS A COURSE ARTICULATION AGREEMENT?

"Course articulation agreements" are agreements between two college systems that courses or sequences of courses at one college will be accepted to fulfill requirements at another college.

Do all colleges have course articulation agreements with each other?

No. To find out if the community college your child will attend has an articulation agreement with a UC or CSU campus, check out www.assist.org. *If your child is going to be a transfer student, it is imperative that he makes an appointment with a transfer center counselor at his community college in the fall semester his first year.*

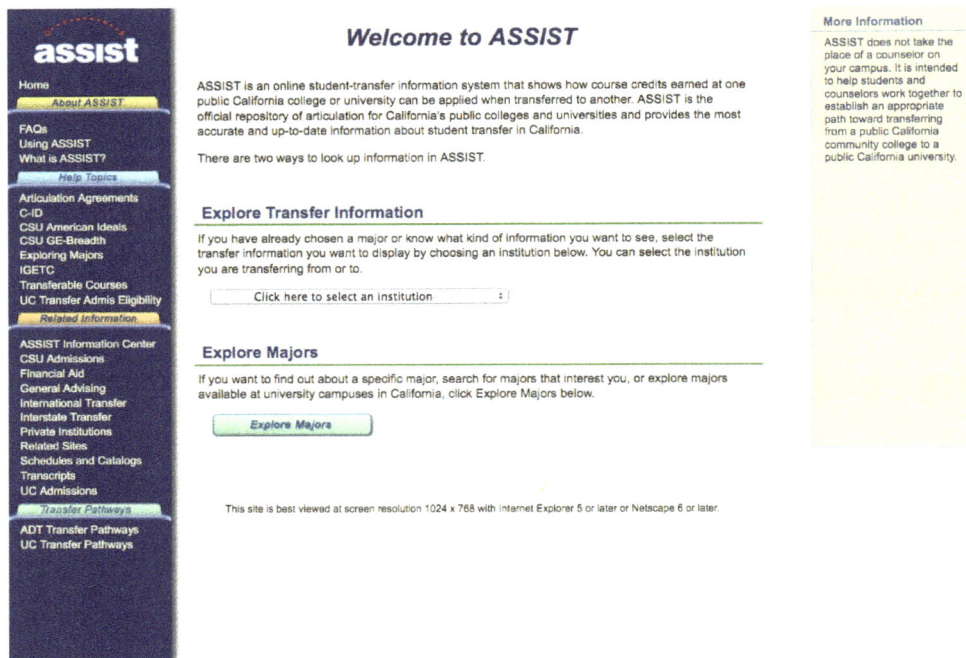

Figure 19 Research Articulation Agreements on ASSIST

COST SAVINGS

If your child completes the first two years of transferable courses at a California community college and then transfers to and completes the final two years of courses at a four-year university or college, your family can save thousands of dollars in tuition, fees, and often room and board.

CSU TRANSFER ADMISSION REQUIREMENTS

All California State University campuses welcome applications from transfer students. The majority of transfer students enter as juniors, or "upper-division transfers." Upper-division transfer students must complete at least 60 semester or 90 quarter units before transferring to a CSU campus.

If your child has completed fewer college units than noted above, he is considered a lower-division transfer. Most CSU campuses do not accept lower-division transfers, so be sure to check with the specific campus if he is considering applying as a lower-division student.

Admission offices at the twenty-three CSU campuses use a common set of factors to make admission decisions for transfer students. Some campuses have higher standards for particular majors.

CSU Transfer Requirements

If your child will have at least 60 semester or 90 quarter transferable units completed by the time he applies to a CSU campus, he is considered an upper-division applicant. To make admission decisions, CSU admissions offices look at the following factors:

- College grades
- The college coursework completed, especially in general education, including four courses that include one course in oral communication, one in written communication, one in critical thinking, and one in quantitative reasoning.
- Academic standing at the last college or university attended

** The Associate Degree for Transfer (AA-T or AS-T) is a special, relatively new degree offered at California community colleges. To pursue this special degree rather than a traditional AA or AS degree, students should meet with a counselor to develop an education plan. The CSU provides certain guarantees to students earning an AA-T or AS-T degree and who meet the CSU minimum eligibility requirements.

Transfer GPA Requirement

Grades are obviously an important factor in CSU admission as an upper-division transfer applicant. To be considered as a CSU upper-division transfer applicant, your child must have a minimum of 60 semester or 90 quarter units and his overall grade point average must be at least 2.0. The GPA is calculated using all transferrable coursework attempted.

Within his transferable courses, there must be 30 units of general education work. Typically, your child will complete at least 10 general education courses. If he is applying to an impacted major, be sure to check with the specific CSU campus for its requirements in this major area.

General education courses in written communication, oral communication, critical thinking, and mathematics (quantitative reasoning) must be completed with a grade of C or better for each course. These four courses are part of the 30 semester units of general education.

Remember, these are the minimums. In the case of high-demand campuses or popular majors with high demand, a 2.0 GPA may not be high enough to be admitted.

UC TRANSFER ADMISSION REQUIREMENTS

The vast majority of transfer students apply to UC at the junior (third year) level. To be considered for UC admission as a junior, your child must fulfill both of the following:

1. Complete 60 semester (90 quarter) units of transferable college credit with a GPA of at least 2.4. No more than 14 semester (21 quarter) units may be taken Pass/Not Pass.

2. Complete the following course pattern requirements, earning a grade of C or better in each course:

    *   Two transferable college courses in English composition and critical thinking.
    *   One transferable college course in mathematical concepts and quantitative reasoning.

3. Four transferable college courses chosen from at least two of the following subject areas:

    *   Arts and humanities
    *   Social and behavioral sciences
    *   Physical and biological sciences

Keep in mind that meeting these requirements does not guarantee admission to the UC campus or major of a student's choice. UC campuses receive more applications than they have spaces available. To be competitive, your child should work toward meeting the specific requirements for the campuses and majors he is interested in, and strive to earn the best grades possible.

Be certain that your child consults many times with a transfer counselor at his community college. The transfer counselor will consult the ASSIST website to ensure that every course your child takes is transferable to the UC system. In addition, your child should visit each UC campus admission website to understand what is required to be competitive for admission to his specific major area.

UC Major Preparation Requirements

Major preparation requirements specify the exact courses your child must take during his first two years of community college to prepare for advanced study in his major. These courses may be required as part of the major, be prerequisites for other courses that are required as part of the major, or be required to gain admission to the major, or all of the above. Transfer applicants are evaluated, in part, on the basis of their performance in major preparation coursework. So it's important—very important—that your child investigates the requirements for his intended UC major as soon as possible. For example, if his major requires specific courses in mathematics and science, it is essential that he completes those prerequisite courses before he transfers. Lack of preparatory coursework may affect his admission to his major, particularly if there are many applicants vying for a limited number of spaces.

IMPORTANT TRANSFER STUDENT INFORMATION

Start Coursework Early

Your child should begin coursework in his major as soon as he has selected one. If he is applying for transfer admissions for fall of the next academic year, the UC campus may require him to complete certain major preparation requirements by the end of his final spring term at the community college. He may also be required to complete general English and Mathematics requirements by a certain time frame prior to his admission to UC.

UC TAP and TAG programs

UC has designed an online tool to help prospective UC transfer students from California Community colleges track and plan their coursework. The UC transfer Admission Planner (UC TAP) can be started from the very beginning of a student's college career. You and your child can access the UC TAP at http://uctap.universityofcalifornia.edu. This planner helps students track their progress toward meeting UC's minimum requirements and allows UC staff to communicate important messages, but does not replace the transfer advising students receive at their community college. The UC TAP is home to UC's unique Transfer Admission Guarantee (TAG) program.

TRANSFER ADMISSION GUARANTEE PROGRAM

The TAG—Transfer Admission Guarantee Program—is offered by six of the nine UC campuses; Berkeley, San Diego, and UCLA do not offer the guarantee. The TAG program guarantee's admission to transfer students who follow the course taking and grade expectation set forth in the TAG agreement. It's important to note that transfer students do not have to participate in TAG to be considered for UC admission. Encourage your child to read the UC campus-specific TAG information very carefully, and to meet with a California community college transfer at his college to stay on track with the TAG requirements.

Important note: Even if your child is approved for a TAG, he must still complete and submit the UC application during the regular admission filing period, which is November 1–30, and meet all conditions of admissions.

Research, research, research!

Encourage your child to check out the transfer preparation paths on the ASSIST website to discover how best to prepare for UC's most popular majors. The "Exploring Majors" feature on www.assist.org lists major-preparation requirements for all UC programs. The lists are updated throughout the year, so check the site periodically to ensure your child has the most current information. The Exploring Majors site can be accessed directly at: http://www2.assist.org/exploring-majors/Welcome.do.

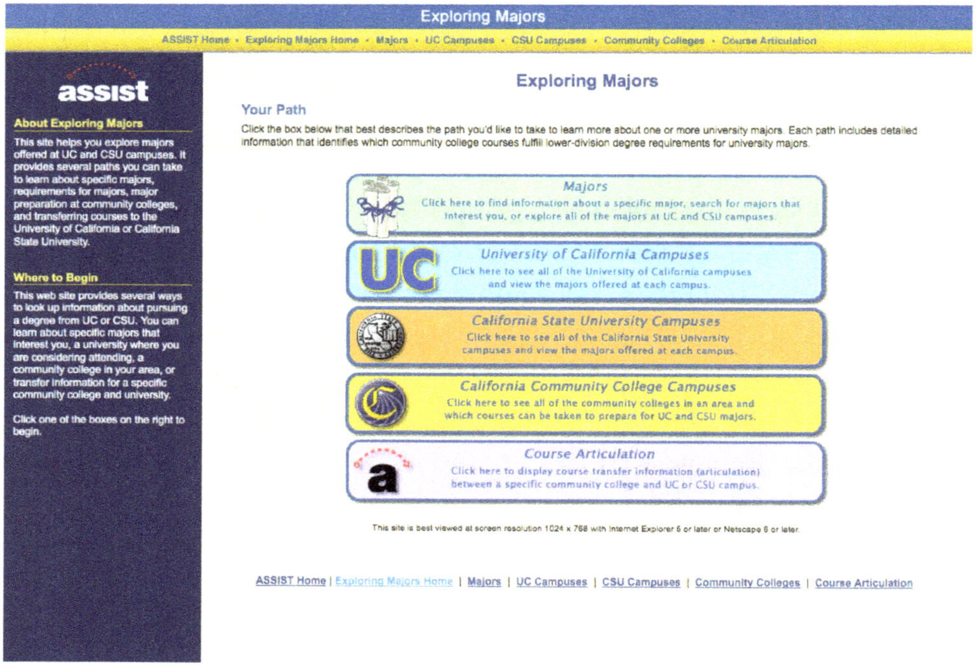

Figure 20   Exploring Majors Site

GENERAL EDUCATION REQUIREMENTS FOR UC TRANSFER STUDENTS

General education (GE) requirements are designed to give UC students a broad background in all major academic disciplines—natural sciences, physical sciences, social sciences, humanities, and fine arts. The general education requirement—(also called the breadth requirement)—lists the specific courses students must take or number of credit hours they must earn in each discipline.

GE Pattern and Course Requirements Can Vary at Each UC Campus

Each UC campus has its own general education requirements. With careful planning, your child can meet many of the lower-division course requirements before he transfers. If he attends a California community college, he also has the option of completing the Intersegmental General Education Transfer Curriculum (IGETC) to satisfy the lower-division general education requirements at a UC campus. More information on IGETC can be found at: http://www.assist.org/web-assist/help/ help-igetc.html.

Entry-Level Writing Requirement

Your child must satisfy an entry-level writing requirement to graduate from any UC campus. One way to meet this requirement is to complete a transferable college course of three semester units in English composition with a grade of C or better. Students who meet the basic requirements for transfer eligibility, which include two transferable college courses in English composition, satisfy the entry-level writing requirement.

Many transfer students can fulfill this requirement while in high school by achieving minimum scores on the following tests or taking advanced level courses:

- Score of 3 on the College Board Advanced Placement (AP) Examination in English (Language or Literature)
- Score of 5 on the International Baccalaureate (IB) Higher-Level Examination in English (Language A only)
- Score of 6 on the IB Standard-Level Examination in English (Language A only)
- Score of 30 on the ACT Plus Writing test or 680 on the Writing section of the SAT Reasoning Test
- While in high school, completing college transferable English courses—three semesters with a grade of "C" or higher, will satisfy this requirement.

Students who have not satisfied the entry-level writing requirement before transferring must complete an appropriate English course at UC.

GPA Requirement for UC Transfer Admission

Your child's grade point average is only one factor UC campuses will use to evaluate him for admissions. Other factors, such as course patterns and major preparation, will also be considered. The average grade point average (GPA) of transfer applicants varies widely by campus and by major. The "Profiles of UC Transfer Students" can give you an idea of the average GPA of admitted transfer students at each UC campus. These profiles can be found at http:// admission. universityofcalifornia.edu/counselors/transfer/profiles%20/.

PRIVATE COLLEGES/UNIVERSITIES TRANSFER ADMISSION REQUIREMENTS

As mentioned in Chapter 8, California is home to seventy-six AICCU accredited private colleges and universities. These colleges often focus on the individual student, and because each college and university is unique, their admissions requirements vary. Similar to freshmen applicants, private college transfer applicants are evaluated on past achievement, future promise, and "fit" with the college's mission and goals. All applicants are treated as individuals and are personally evaluated by an admissions officer.

Generally, transfer admission requirements at private colleges and universities fall into four categories: (1) admission requirements similar to the University of California; (2) admission requirements similar to the California State University system; (3) admission requirements that accept only the top 10 percent of transfer students; and (4) very specific admission requirements— in addition to a well-rounded curriculum—related to their specialty, for example, experience in the visual or performing arts.

The terms "private" and "independent" are used interchangeably to describe colleges and universities that are not supported by state funding, and therefore can be much more wide-ranging in their admissions policies. Although many transfer students think that they will not be able to afford an education at a private college, often they receive financial aid packages that compare favorably with those from public colleges and universities. Transferring to a private college from a community college can sometimes be more involved than transferring to a CSU or UC campus. Usually, applicants need to write a personal essay, fill out a more detailed application form, and may need to include writing samples from class work. Private colleges have different deadlines for transfer admissions applications and financial aid, so it is crucial to be well-informed about each college's policies, and to complete applications in a timely manner.

It is imperative that your child do the following if he is planning to apply as a transfer student to a private college:

- Initiate contact right away by e-mailing or calling the college and asking for a transfer application packet. He can find e-mail addresses and phone numbers by looking through the college's website. Most private colleges have online transfer applications on their websites or PDF applications for students to download and print.

- Read the transfer application carefully to find out what the application deadlines are, the topic for the personal essay, and other requirements such as writing samples, video, or audio tapes of performances or interviews.

Find out if your child needs to obtain written recommendations from teachers and/or counselors.

Many California independent colleges have course articulation agreements with California community colleges. However, course-to-course articulation between the community college and the private/independent school is not always available, so have your child work with his transfer counselor early for help in deciding what classes to take for that specific private college.

Chapter 10

Financial Aid

"An investment in knowledge pays the best interest."
—Benjamin Franklin

Probably one of the first questions in your minds about college is, how are we going to pay for it? In this chapter, we will outline the many financial aid resources available to your family to help fund your child's college education. Almost every family will need some type of assistance in order to cover the high cost of a college education, regardless of income or your child's choice of college. In 2014, more than 63 percent of all college students working toward a bachelor's degree received some sort of financial aid. (Source: U.S. Department of Education, National Center for Education Statistics, 2014.)

There are several sources of financial aid that, together, can help your child attend and graduate from the college of her choice.

FINANCIAL AID TERMS EXPLAINED

"Financial Aid" is money to help pay for the costs of higher education, whether the education is at a community college, four-year public institution, private university, or trade school. This money can come from the U.S. government, the state of California, the college your child plans to attend, and/or private sources. The most important thing to remember is that your child has to apply for financial aid <u>every year</u> she's enrolled in college in order to receive aid.

Financial aid can help with the following costs:

- Tuition and fees
- Room and board
- Books and supplies (may include a computer)

- Transportation costs
- Personal expenses: cell phone, health care, clothing, personal necessities, laundry, toiletries, etc.

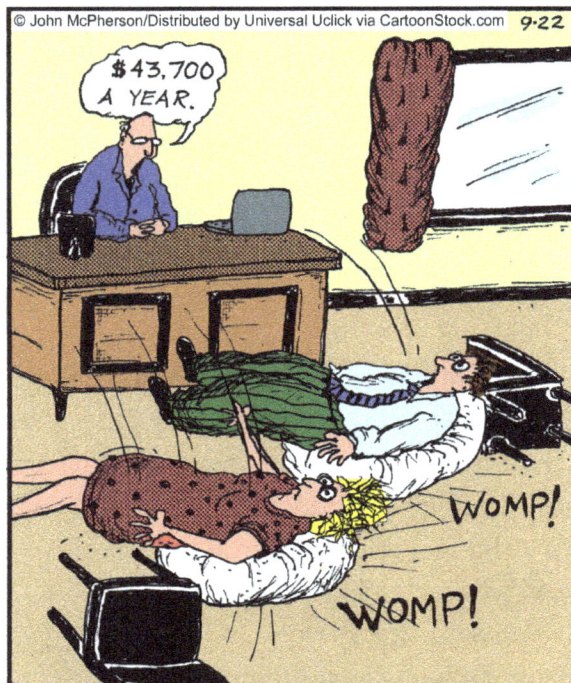

For their safety, many colleges require that parents put on airbags before they are told what the school's tuition is.

STATE AND FEDERAL GOVERNMENT FINANCIAL AID PROGRAMS

Grant Programs

Grants are "free" money, and do not have to be paid back. Grants typically come from the federal or state government. Why does the government want to use tax money toward financial aid? It is in the best interest of the state to have its residents educated and/or trained in order to be gainfully employed and become future taxpaying citizens. Government grants are very carefully regulated and have strict guidelines for funding. By using taxpayer dollars for financial aid, the government is investing in your child. Grants are based on a family's determined financial need—therefore the less money your family has, the more likely your child will qualify for government grants. Grants tend to be focused on lower-income and

middle-income students. The two most common government grants awarded to college students in California are the state Cal Grant and the federal Pell Grant. These grants DO NOT have to be repaid. California awards the following four state grants: BOG Fee Waiver, Cal Grant A, Cal Grant B, and Cal Grant C, all for approved California schools only.

BOG Fee Waiver

The Board of Governors (BOG) Fee Waiver is a program that provides assistance to cover community college enrollment fees for students from low- to middle-income families. The BOG is worth up to approximately $1,400 a year. No money is awarded directly, instead students' course fees are waived each semester if they are awarded this fee waiver.

Cal Grant A

Cal Grant A is a grant that can be used for tuition and fees at public and private colleges. The award limits for Cal Grant A in 2018–2019 school year are:

- CSU—$5,742
- UC—$12,630
- Private—$9,084

Cal Grant A is a grant for lower to middle-income students with a minimum 3.0 high school GPA, or 2.4 college GPA if transferring to a four-year college from a California community college. These awards help pay tuition and fees at qualifying schools with academic programs that are at least two years in length. In the 2018–2019 school year, Cal Grant A will pay up to $9,084 toward tuition and fees at private California colleges and universities.

Cal Grant A is not awarded to students at community colleges. These students receive the BOG fee waiver instead.

Cal Grant B

Cal Grant B is awarded to students with a minimum 2.0 GPA who are from low-income families, and can be awarded to community college students, unlike Cal Grant A. This grant provides low-income students with a living allowance and assistance with tuition and fees. In the 2018–2019 academic year, an allowance of up to $1,672 for books and living expenses was awarded to students. If the student is attending a four-year school, after the freshman year, Cal Grant B also helps pay tuition and fees in the same dollar amount as a Cal Grant A. For a Cal Grant B, your child's college program must be at least one academic year in length.

The Middle Class Scholarship (MCS)

- The Middle Class Scholarship (MCS) provides undergraduate students, including students pursuing a teaching credential, with family incomes and assets up to $156,000 a scholarship to attend University of California (UC) or California State University (CSU) campuses.

- Students must meet the following requirements: be a California resident attending a UC or CSU; be a U.S. citizen, permanent resident or have AB 540* student status; meet certain income/asset and other financial aid standards; maintain satisfactory academic progress; not be in default on a student loan; and, must not be incarcerated.

- Eligibility for the MCS is limited to 4 years.

- Beginning on October 1st, students may complete a Free Application for Federal Student Aid (FAFSA) online at www.fafsa.gov or the California Dream Act Application (CADAA) at www.caldreamact.org. Use the California Dream Act Application if you do not have a Social Security number (SSN) or if you have a Deferred Action for Childhood Arrivals (DACA) number. Make sure your email address is listed on your FAFSA or CADAA. The deadline to apply is March 2nd.

- After you have submitted your FAFSA or CADAA establish a www.webgrants4 students.org account to monitor your state financial aid.

- Students whose families earn between $104,001 and $156,000 per year may be eligible for a scholarship of no less than 10 percent and no more than 40% of the mandatory system-wide tuition and fees at the University of California and the California State University.

- MCS scholarships are not set amounts and may vary by student and institution. The award is amount is determined after you are awarded any federal, state, and institutional need-based grants for which you are eligible. The final award amount will be based on the number of students eligible for the MCS statewide and the funding allocated by the State Budget.

- To get assistance completing the FAFSA or CADAA, attend a Cash for College workshop in your community beginning on October 1st but before the March 2nd application deadline. Students must reapply each year. Visit www.cash4college.org or download our mobile app at www.mobilegallery.ca.gov for workshop locations.

- If you are selected to receive a MCS, you will be notified by the California Student Aid Commission.

- If you need more information about this scholarship contact your UC or CSU campus Financial Aid Office or check your www.webgrants4students.org account.

Other Government Programs That Assist with College Costs

There are several other state and federal programs that can help with college costs. Be sure to visit the following sites for more information about these programs.

Dream Act   A new law, the California Dream Act of 2011, allows students who meet AB 540** criteria to apply for and receive non-state funded scholarships for public colleges and universities, receive state-funded financial aid such as college grants, community college fee waivers, the Cal Grant, and the Chafee Grant. If your child is not a U.S. citizen or a permanent resident, she should submit the California Dream application, located at www.csac.ca.gov/dream_act.asp.

**What is AB 540?

On October 12, 2011, the state of California created a new exemption from the payment of non-resident tuition for certain non-resident students who have attended high school in California and received a high school diploma or its equivalent. For guidelines, refer to: http://ab540.com/What_Is_AB540_.html.

Foster Youth   The Chafee Grant for Foster Youth is available to current and former foster care youth to pay for tuition, books, housing, and transportation. Visit https://www.chafee.csac.ca.gov/ for more information.

AmeriCorps   This non-military domestic community service program provides assistance with college costs and provides awards to participants who successfully complete service of one to two years. Awards can be used for college expenses or to pay back student loans. For more information, visit www.nationalservice.gov/programs/americorps.

U.S. Service Academies   The U.S. Air Force, U.S. Army, U.S. Coast Guard, U.S. Merchant Marine, and U.S. Navy provide a free college education for a highly select group of students who commit to serve for a certain period of time in the military during and upon completion of their college education. For more information, go to http://todaysmilitary.com/training/service-academies-and-military-colleges.

Reserve Officer Training Corps (ROTC)   This college campus-based program offers scholarships in varying amounts to students interested in serving in the military after college. For more information, go to www.todaysmilitary.com/training/rotc.

GI Bill   Men and women who enlist and serve in the armed forces may apply for and receive direct financial assistance to attend college. This program may also provide financial aid to spouses and dependents of veterans. Go to www.benefits.va.gov/gibill/ for more information.

SCHOLARSHIPS

What Is a Scholarship?

A scholarship is "free" money awarded by private individuals, businesses, community organizations, foundations, and colleges. Most scholarships are based on either financial need or merit. "Merit" means the scholarship is based on a particular ability your child has, such as sports, music, or grades or based on her participation in a particular activity such as community service, student clubs, etc.

Scholarships can be awarded one time, or can be "renewed" for each year your child is in college. However, some scholarships will require that a certain grade point average (GPA) is maintained while receiving scholarship funds. There are literally thousands of scholarships out there. How does my child apply for scholarships?

You have probably heard that thousands of dollars of scholarships go unclaimed every year. Add to that the fact that many outstanding students do not get scholarships each year. The fact is, there are thousands of scholarships available. Many of them, however, have very specific eligibility criteria.

Students generally must have an outstanding GPA (3.5 or better), high ACT/SAT scores, and excellent recommendations in order to receive most "merit-based" academic scholarships. A student must be <u>exceptionally talented</u> in order to receive an athletic scholarship. Other scholarships are based on criteria such as being the first in the family to attend college or involvement in an extracurricular activity.

Students who are willing to invest the time and energy into scholarship applications often find that their efforts pay off. When looking for scholarships, START EARLY. Start researching scholarship applications during the last two years of high school, and encourage your child to locate and complete applications no later than the fall of her senior year.

Steps for Researching and Applying for Scholarships

1. Start the scholarship search by having your child create a MyFAFSA account at www. studentaid.ed.gov/scholarship in order to use the Financial Aid and Scholarship Wizard.

2. A great site for researching scholarships for California students is: https://secure.cali-forniacolleges.edu/Financial_Aid_ Planning/_default.aspx.

3. Look at your child's first and second choice colleges and find the web link to their financial aid/scholarship offices for more information about how to apply for scholarships at that particular college.

4. Private colleges are often more generous when awarding scholarships. Don't rule out a private college *without seeing* its financial aid and scholarship award letter.

5. Apply for scholarships from local groups and organizations such as Rotary, PTA, Elks, etc. These scholarships are generally for smaller amounts ($100–$1,000), but they are usually easier to apply for and to receive.

6. Take note that scholarship applications become available throughout a student's senior year.

7. Ask, ask, ask! Let your child's high school counselor know that you're looking for scholarships for your child. Ask about scholarship opportunities with your place of employment and with any local organizations to which you belong.

8. High school counseling centers, offices, career centers, and libraries have books and computer programs that list scholarship opportunities.

9. Make sure that teachers and counselors are given plenty of time to write recommendations for your child and to prepare transcripts. Be aware of deadlines!

10. Remember that most financial aid is NOT awarded in the form of a scholarship. It is critical that your child submits a financial aid application (FAFSA or California Dream Application) during EVERY year that she is in college.

11. Always check to see if financial aid and scholarship awards are renewable. A one-year scholarship is for one year only but a renewable scholarship can become a four-year scholarship if your child keeps her grades up.

12. The Federal Trade Commission estimates that hundreds of thousands of families are scammed out of millions of dollars each year by fraudulent companies. Beware! You should NEVER pay money to a company for a scholarship or financial aid.

13. The scholarship services listed below are free and they provide excellent information. They match a student's interests, plans, background, and special circumstances with thousands of government, community, and campus-based scholarship programs.

   • www.petersons.com

   • www.collegeboard.com

   • www.fastweb.com

14. Ensure that your child's application is completed in full and that her name is on every page of an application. Make sure that everything the application has requested (essay, transcript, recommendation, etc.) is included, and make a copy before mailing or uploading the application documents.

Athletic Scholarships

As discussed in Chapter 5, if your child plays sports in high school and desires to go after a scholarship to continue to play sports in college, the first place to start is with a reality check. If your child has her heart set on playing Division I college sports, be sure to make her aware of the following: The reality is that a very low percentage of high school players nationwide end up playing sports in college. According to www.scholarshipstats.com, in 2013–14, the breakdown of high school athletes accepted to play at the college level was the following:

- Basketball—5.9 percent of high school males and 6.3 percent of high school female athletes.
- Soccer—8.9 percent of high school males and 9.6 percent of high school female athletes.
- Baseball—11.2 percent of high school male athletes.
- Softball—7.8 percent of high school female athletes.
- Football—7.8 percent of high school male athletes.

These are not great odds. If your child is still interested in pursuing sports in college, consider guiding your child in the following ways, starting no later than the beginning of your child's junior year:

- Obtain a realistic assessment of your child's athletic talent. This talent assessment will help you determine the appropriate level of play for her at the college level. Do not rule out NAIA or NCAA Division II and III colleges if they can help your child attain his/her academic goals. Casting a wide net will improve her chance of being successfully recruited.
- Talk with your child's school counselor to make sure your child is following the National Collegiate Athletic Association (NCAA) rules (www.ncaa.org).
- Have a realistic expectation with respect to available athletic scholarship money. In addition to athletic scholarships, many colleges offer other types of financial assistance

and the pool of available money may be substantially increased if your child has strong academic grades and test scores.

- Some colleges do not offer athletic scholarships, or need to allocate scarce scholarship money to more players than their program is funded to carry. It is not uncommon in smaller schools, or less prominent sports programs at larger schools, for scholarships to cover only a portion of the costs associated with attending college. However, your child can supplement her total financial package through other forms of financial aid such as academic grants, scholarships, and/or student loans.

- If your child is being considered for an athletic scholarship, be certain to check on the graduation rates of the college's athletes against the graduation rates of all of the students at that college.

Now that you know a little about the types of financial aid available, let's talk about the costs of college.

UNDERSTANDING THE COST OF ATTENDANCE (COA) AT EACH COLLEGE OR UNIVERSITY

It is critical to note that the Cost of Attendance (COA) at each college or university varies greatly. All colleges factor in the following components to arrive at the estimated cost for a student to attend THEIR college or university for one year.

The five components included in the COA are:

1. Tuition & fees
2. Housing and Food (also called "Room and Board")
3. Books & supplies
4. Transportation to and from your child's home
5. Personal expenses

The COA is different for EVERY college, and each college has a different COA depending on a student's housing plans (for example: living with parents, living off-campus, or living in on-campus housing).

It is very important to note that your child should be prepared to have a great deal of control over how much money she spends on expenses. Therefore, if she is careful and can spend less than what the college estimates she will need, then her overall personalized COA will be lower than the college's estimated COA.

RESEARCHING COLLEGE COSTS: AN EXERCISE FOR YOUR COLLEGE-BOUND STUDENT

This exercise will be helpful during your child's junior or senior year. It will help her understand the cost of college, and assist with researching the actual cost of her favorite college(s). To complete this exercise, instruct your child to use the following chart (also located in the Appendix):

Worksheet Instructions

1. Locate each college's website. Your child can then create her own personalized COA Worksheet by following these directions.

2. Under the "School's Estimate" column, enter the dollar values found on the college's website for the following information:
   - Tuition/fees.
   - Room/board (usually, this amount is listed as a single dollar value, just put the number in the field for "Room" and leave the field for "Board" blank).
   - Books/supplies.
   - Computer costs (this is usually NOT included in the COA, so the number in the School's Estimate column will be "0").
   - Transportation.
   - Personal (this might be called "Miscellaneous" on the college's website)—the college will NOT break this down into "Clothing, Laundry, Cell Phone, Medical, etc."—it will be listed as a single dollar value.

3. Under the "My Expectation" column, enter the information that is more personalized to your child's expectations. You might need to help your child with this column.

4. Tuition/fees—This amount will be the same as the School's Estimate.

5. Room/board—This amount will vary depending on where your child plans to live (on-campus, off-campus, or with parents). Books/Supplies—If your child will have a highly technical major like art, engineering, or biology, then her expenses in this category will likely be about the same as the college's estimate. Although these costs can be high, there are also several ways to obtain discounts on textbooks. More information on where to find discounted textbooks can be found at http://www.bookfinder.com/textbooks/.

NASFAA
NATIONAL ASSOCIATION OF STUDENT FINANCIAL AID ADMINISTRATORS

COST OF ATTENDANCE COMPARISON WORKSHEET

The actual cost of attendance (COA) is unique for each student at each school. While some expenses are fixed (like tuition and fees), others are influenced and controlled by the student's lifestyle (like housing and personal expenses). When considering the award package from a particular school, or in comparing packages from multiple schools, you can use this worksheet to compare your cost expectations to each school's estimated total COA. The goal of this comparison is to better decide if the resulting difference is realistically manageable given the resources available to your family and the aid being offered by each school. Copy this worksheet as needed.

School	1.		2.		3.	
	My Expectation	School's Estimate	My Expectation	School's Estimate	My Expectation	School's Estimate
Tuition and Fees	$	$	$	$	$	$
Room	$	$	$	$	$	$
Board	$	$	$	$	$	$
Books and Supplies	$	$	$	$	$	$
Computer Costs	$	$	$	$	$	$
Transportation	$	$	$	$	$	$
Personal:						
Clothing	$	$	$	$	$	$
Laundry	$	$	$	$	$	$
Medical	$	$	$	$	$	$
Entertainment	$	$	$	$	$	$
Other_____	$	$	$	$	$	$
Other_____	$	$	$	$	$	$
Other_____	$	$	$	$	$	$
Total COA	$	$	$	$	$	$
Difference between my expectation and school's estimate	$		$		$	

Figure 22   Cost of College Attendance Comparison Worksheet

6. Technology Costs—If your child does not have a computer then list the amount for a decent laptop (around $600).

7. Transportation:

   - If your child already has a car, how much will it cost to insure, maintain, and pay for gas for a year? If she plans to park on campus, then research how much it will cost to pay for a campus parking permit. (Note that some colleges do not allow students to bring a car to campus during their freshman year.)

   - If your child does not need a car, then research how much it will cost for your child to get to and from the campus on a daily basis.

   - If your child will move away from home, research how much it will cost for them to travel between home and the college for holidays and school breaks (bus, plane, train, or carpool with other local students).

8. Personal Expenses: Think about how much you spend on each of these categories for your child on an annual basis. Include Internet and cell phone charges.

9. After filling in the categories on the worksheet, ask the following questions: Is there a difference between the college's estimated "sticker price" (COA) and your child's personalized COA?

10. Is your child's personalized COA higher or lower than the college's estimated COA? It is about the same overall, but different in individual categories?

HOW DOES YOUR CHILD OBTAIN FINANCIAL AID TO HELP COVER COLLEGE COSTS?

After October 1 and before March 2 of your child's senior year of high school, you and your child should complete and submit a Free Application for Federal Student Aid (FAFSA) located at www.fafsa.gov.

(Please Note: If your child is NOT a U.S. citizen or a permanent resident, she should submit the California Dream application, located at www.csac.ca.gov/dream_act.asp.)

What Is the FAFSA?

- Free Application for Federal Student Aid—To be considered for federal, state, and institutional aid, a student must complete a FAFSA. It collects financial and other information used to calculate your family's expected family contribution (EFC). The EFC is a measure of how much the student and his or her family can be expected to contribute.

- Gateway to financial aid—Although FAFSA's calculations are designed primarily to determine a student's "need-based" financial aid requirement, it is often used as a factor in determining "merit-based" grants and scholarships as well. What exactly does the FAFSA measure?

1. Assets—Both parents' and student's assets. The FAFSA calculation does not include equity in a home or the value of any retirement programs such as an IRA, 401K, 401b. However, 529 plans are included as parent assets when they are in the parent's name. The calculation also does not include specific documented assets associated with a small business, farm, or ranch.

2. Income—Both parents' and student's income. All sources of income including welfare, private insurance disability, and possibly Social Security may be included.

3. Number of students in college—If a parent is attending college as well as the parent's child, the parent can claim the student, but the student cannot claim the parent.

4. Age of oldest parent—The closer a parent or student is to retirement, the less effect their assets will have.

5. Number of family members in household.

What Is the FAFSA Process and How Does It Work?

Students file a FAFSA online beginning October 1st and before March 2 of each year, beginning the application in the fall of their senior year of high school.

- The FAFSA information is automatically transmitted to the college(s) of your student's choice.

- The colleges then use the information from the FAFSA to determine an EFC (Expected Family Contribution) from the five measures listed previously. The EFC is a description of a family's/student's expected contribution to the college's annual cost of attendance (COA).

- Example: 2016–17 COA (cost of attendance) at XYZ University:

Tuition	$15,000
Books/Materials	$1,500
Room & Board	$10,000
Transportation	$1,200
Incidentals/Misc.	$2,500
Other Fees	$800
Total COA	$31,000

After the FAFSA is submitted the student will receive a Student Aid Report (SAR) via e-mail. This report is an opportunity to correct any mistakes or make adjustments, so that the colleges have the most recent and correct information regarding your child's financial circumstances.

Financial Aid Application Instructions

For 12th Grade Students and Their Families Only

Use the following steps to assist your senior student with her financial aid application during October of her senior year in high school.

Step One—Complete the Free Application for Federal Student Aid (FAFSA) or the California Dream Application

The online FAFSA application can be found at http://fafsa.ed.gov.

You will need to set up an FSA ID for the student and one parent. This can be done at https://fsaid.ed.gov. Be sure to save all User Names, Passwords, and Challenge Questions in one safe location for the entire period your child is in college.

The FAFSA or California Dream Act application should first be completed in October of your child's senior year in high school.

Try to submit the FAFSA as close to October 1 as possible, as some financial aid is awarded on a first-come, first-served basis. Most importantly, file the FAFSA before the deadline of March 2.

The FAFSA application requests information about your family's income and assets to generate an "Expected Family Contribution" or EFC for your child. This EFC is used as the basis for determining your child's financial need. You will need to have your most recent tax forms and other financial information readily available when completing the FAFSA with your child.

Again, if you live in California and your child is not a U.S. citizen or a permanent resident, do not fill out the FAFSA. Instead talk to your school counselor to see if your student meets AB540 criteria and can apply for the California Dream Application at www.csac.ca.gov/dream_act.asp.

Important Tip

The first "F" in FAFSA stands for "free" so you should not pay to complete or submit it! EVERY graduating high school and college student should submit a FAFSA every year, no matter what college they are applying to or how much money their parents earn.

Step Two—Submit your child's GPA to the Cal Grant system

California students must submit their Cal Grant GPA by March 2 of their senior year. Many high schools do this automatically. Check with your high school counselor.

Step Three—File additional financial aid paperwork with specific college(s)

Community Colleges

Community colleges in California award thousands of Board of Governors (BOG) Fee Waivers every year. If your child is planning on attending a community college, the application for the BOG fee waiver must be submitted to the college's financial aid office, in addition to the FAFSA. This application for a fee waiver is available in early spring at the financial aid office at all community colleges. If your child qualifies, she does not have to pay the unit fee to take college classes. (In 2015–16, the unit fee was $46 per unit.)

Private Colleges

If your child plans to attend a private college or university, some of these colleges require the CSS/Financial Aid PROFILE. The CSS PROFILE is merely another financial aid document that goes into further detail regarding your child's financial circumstances. If required, the CSS/Financial Aid PROFILE can be found on the financial aid link at each of the private colleges to which your child applies. Contact the financial aid office as soon as possible if your child is applying to private colleges to find out if the CSS PROFILE is required, or go online to https://student.collegeboard.org/css-financial-aid-profile.

Step Four—Research and apply for ALL POSSIBLE scholarships

Thousands of scholarships are available for students with varying GPAs and who are planning to attend almost every type of college or trade school. Scholarship research and submission requires work and time but it does pay off for students who apply early and often. Tell your child to treat applying for scholarships like a part-time job that will eventually pay off, and then follow the steps outlined (starting on page 187).

Step Five—Check with your college (s) to see if any verification paperwork is required

Some colleges may ask you to submit specific paperwork to "verify FAFSA information" or CSS/PROFILE information. Turn in this paperwork as soon as possible.

Step Six—Do not fear student loans

With the high cost of college today, most students will receive student loans as a part of their financial aid package(s). Student loans awarded through the FAFSA are considered financial aid since they are awarded without a credit check or any type of collateral, and at a low interest rate. The majority of these federal loans do not require any type of repayment until the student stops attending college or graduates from college.

Federally subsidized loans are very different from private loans. Be careful; make sure you talk to the financial aid office at the college your child plans to attend before you take out any private loans, as many of these loans require repayment within ninety days and also charge high interest rates.

Student loans are useful in helping pay college costs, but be sure to consider the total amount your child may need to borrow over the course of her college career. In the future, those loans will have to be repaid.

Step Seven—Budget

Most students will need to take out some form of student loan to help pay for their college education. These loans are needed, but they also need to be repaid, and will not be forgiven down the road, even if a person files for bankruptcy. If your child is taking out a loan, be certain to create and stick to a realistic budget for her time in college, and limit her loans accordingly. Write out a concrete plan for how she will pay back these loans once she has graduated, and make sure she is involved in every step of the process.

UNDERSTANDING HOW COLLEGES ESTIMATE FINANCIAL NEED

Each college will consider all of the information gathered from your child's FAFSA or California Dream Act application to estimate your child's financial need.

Financial Need is calculated using the following:

Cost of Attendance (COA) – (minus) Expected Family Contribution (EFC) = Financial Need

UNDERSTANDING THE EXPECTED FAMILY CONTRIBUTION (EFC)

- The Estimated Family Contribution (EFC) is the amount the federal government determines that your family can contribute to your child's college costs on an annual basis. This amount is calculated using data generated from the FAFSA and is unique for each student and their family income situation. Additional facts about the EFC include the following:
- The EFC calculation stays the same regardless of the type of college your child plans to attend. If her EFC is $467, it will be $467 at a community college, it will be $467 at a four-year public university, and it will be $467 at a private school.
- The EFC is the measure of what your family can contribute to your child's college costs for one academic year. The EFC has two portions: a parent portion and a student portion.
- The EFC is calculated from information you entered into the FAFSA: parental income and assets, student's income and assets, number of people in the household, number of college students in the household, and other factors.
- The EFC is unique for each student. One student may have an EFC of $1,843, another student may have an EFC of $4,289, and a third may have an EFC of $0. The EFC will be different for every student and can change from year to year depending on the information entered on your child's annual FAFSA or California Dream Act application.

How to Estimate Your Child's Expected Family Contribution

If you would like to get an estimate of what your student's Expected Family Contribution (EFC) might be and also get an idea of how much federal financial aid your child might receive for one year of college, you can use the EFC Calculator at http://www.ecmc.org/My-EFC-Calculator/. You will be asked to enter information about your child's income and assets, your income and assets, your household size, and the number of college students in your household. The EFC Calculator will then generate an estimated EFC and a rough idea of potential federal financial aid for one year. Please note that this is an estimate of the EFC, and the amount of potential federal financial aid does not include possible financial aid from the state of California, the college itself, or possible scholarships.

How the Process Works at Each College

After your child submits the FAFSA or the California Dream Act application, the financial aid office at each college your child applies to will compare the college's COA (Cost of Attendance) to your child's EFC (Estimated Family Contribution) to determine your child's financial need for that college.

Your child's financial need will be different at each college, because the Cost of Attendance is different at each college.

The financial aid office at each college your child applies to will then look at various forms of financial aid and try to fill your child's financial aid "need bucket" so that she receives as much financial aid as possible.

".. . and help my parents to pick the right investments for my college education."

Filling the Financial Aid "Need Bucket"

Financial aid offices will try to meet your child's financial need in the following order:

- Your family's (EFC) contribution

- Government grants—based on need: Pell Grants and Cal Grants—discussed earlier in this chapter

- Institutional (college) grants and scholarships: College grants and scholarships do not have to be paid back

- Federal work-study: Work-study is a specific form of financial aid. If eligible to participate based on financial need, your child will need to find a work/study job on campus and earn the money throughout the year.

- Outside scholarships: These are scholarships that YOUR CHILD has to independently apply for. The more scholarships she applies for, the better her chances for getting more scholarship money. Scholarships do not have to be paid back.

- Loans: The federal government offers three types of student/family loans:

  - Subsidized—The government pays the interest while your child is in college.

  - Unsubsidized—The interest on the loan starts accruing as soon as your child receives the money each term.

- The federal government also has something called a Parent PLUS loan—You as a parent can take out a loan to help your child afford college.

Understanding Financial Aid Award Letters

After you and your child have completed the FAFSA and all other related financial aid documents, each college your child has applied to will then provide her with a "Financial Aid Award Letter" in the spring or summer of her senior year. An award letter will detail all of the financial aid resources that the college can provide. Shown on the following pages are sample award letters. The first letter is an example of a student planning to attend a community college, while the second letter is an example of a student planning to enroll at a four-year California State University (CSU), University of California (UC) campus, or four-year private college or university.

Sample financial award letter—California Community College

Date: 04/15/2016
Student ID number: 1234567
Social Security Number: 555-55-1234
Award Year: 2016–2017

Dear Student,

This is your Financial Aid Award Letter for the 2016–2017 academic year. Awards are based on full-time attendance and will be reduced if you are enrolled in less than 12 units or drop classes during the semester. If you withdraw during the semester you may owe funds back.

Accepting financial aid means that you acknowledge your responsibilities in using funds. View your online account for ongoing communication. Please note that the BOG fee waiver is NOT a cash award. These funds will be applied toward your fees. A BOG fee waiver does not pay for Health, Campus Center or Parking fees.

2016–2017 Budget (Student Living with Parents'):

Fees:	$1,182		
Books/Supplies:	$1,746	Expected Family Contribution	$1,500
Room/Board:	$4,600	Estimated Financial Need:	$10,294
Transportation:	$1,134	Award Total (breakdown below):	$8,732
Personal Expenses:	$3,132	Unmet Need:	$1,562

TOTAL Cost of Attendance: $22,414

Award Type	Total	Fall	Spring
BOG fee waiver	$1,104	$552	$552
Cal Grant A	$1,648	$737	$736
PELL Grant	$4,230	$2,115	$2,115
Outside Scholarship	$250	$250	$0
Federal Work Study	$1,500	$750	$750
TOTAL:	$8,732	$4,491	$4,241

An Explanation of the financial aid award letter for a student attending a California community college is below:

- The student's Expected Family Contribution is $1,500. An EFC of $1,500 means that this family is fairly low-income, yet does have some financial resources to contribute.

- Pell Grant: This grant is for students with the very lowest income.

- Cal Grant: This student qualifies for Cal Grant B. At the community college, the Cal Grant B is worth $1,648.

- BOG fee waiver: This student applied for and qualified for the BOG fee waiver. The waiver is worth a value of approximately $1,104 in 2016–2017.

- Institutional grants and scholarships: Community colleges do have numerous scholarships for students, but at this point, we are assuming your child hasn't heard back yet from the scholarships she applied for through the college.

- Federal work-study: This student is being offered $1,500 in work-study. She will have to apply for a work/study job on campus and work to earn the money over the course of the year.

- Outside scholarships: This student applied for four community scholarships and received one for $250. She spent a total of 10 hours on completing scholarship applications, so she ended up earning $25 an hour. Not a bad return on investment!

- Loans: Community colleges typically do not offer loans, but they are still available through outside sources such as the federal government.

- This student's financial aid award letter breaks down the basic information as follows:
  - Cost of Attendance: $11,794
  - Estimate Family Contribution: $1,500
  - Financial aid offered: $8,732

Sample financial award letter—CSU/UC campus or four-year private college

Date: 04/15/2016
Student ID number: 1234567
Social Security Number: 555-55-1234
Award Year: 2016–207

Dear Student,

This is your Financial Aid Award Letter for the 2016–2017 award year. Awards are based on full-time attendance and will be reduced if you are enrolled in less than 12 units or drop classes during the semester. Accepting financial aid means that you acknowledge your responsibilities in using funds. View your online account for ongoing communication.

2016–2017 Budget (Student Living On-Campus):

Fees:	$7,002		
Books/Supplies:	$1,746	Expected Family Contribution	$4,000
Room/Board:	$11,208	Estimated Financial Need:	$18,414
Transportation:	$1,092	Award Total (breakdown below):	$17,002
Personal Expenses:	$1,366	Unmet Need:	$1,412

TOTAL Cost of Attendance: $22,414

Award Type	Total	Fall	Spring
PELL Grant	$1,730	$865	$865
EOP Grant	$800	$400	$400
Outside Scholarship	$1,000	$500	$500
Outside Scholarship	$250	$250	$0
Outside Scholarship	$250	$250	$0
Federal Work-Study	$2,000	$1,000	$1,000
Fed Direct Loan Sub.	$3,500	$1,750	$1,750
Fed Perkins Loan	$2,000	$1,000	$1,000
Cal Grant A	$5,472	$2,736	$2,736
TOTAL:	$17,002	$8,751	$8,251

An Explanation of the financial aid award letter for a student attending a CSU or UC campus or four-year private institution is below:

- The student's Expected Family Contribution is $4,000. An EFC of $4,000 means that this family is lower-middle income, but does have some resources to help the student.
- Pell Grant: The higher the EFC, the lower the amount of Pell Grant. A student with an EFC of $4,000 could expect to receive approximately $1,730 in Pell Grant funding.
- Cal Grant: This student qualifies for Cal Grant A. Cal Grant A at a CSU campus was worth the amount of CSU fees in 2016–17, or $5,472. ($12,192 if this were a UC sample award letter and $9,223 if this were a private CA college or university sample award letter.)
- Institutional grants and scholarships: This student is a first-generation college student; she applied for the Educational Opportunity Program and was accepted. For the student's first year in college, EOP provides an $800 grant.
- Federal work-study: This student is being offered $2,000 in work-study. She will have to apply for a work-study job on campus and work to earn the money over the course of the year.
- Outside scholarships: This student applied for ten different scholarships and received three scholarships for a total of $1,500. She spent a total of 15 hours on the scholarship applications, so she earned $100 an hour.
- Loans: The student was offered $3,500 in direct subsidized loan and $2,000 in Perkins Loan for a total of $5,500. She will not have to begin to repay these loans until she leaves or graduates from college. Also, the interest on these loans will be paid by the government until she leaves or graduates from college. After all the grants, work study, and loans, the student still has a gap (or unmet need) of $1,412.

Unmet Need

This student has an EFC of $4,000. Therefore, the student/family needs to come up with funds to cover the unmet need of $1,412 plus the $4,000 EFC for a total of $5,412.

How do families address "unmet need"?

Options for how families can address unmet financial needs include:

- Family resources (examples: savings, selling of assets, second mortgages)
- Parent PLUS Loans
- Alternative loans—Private bank or personal loans

CONFUSED YET?

The world of Financial Aid can be daunting, even for those of us in education. To guide you every step of the way, we have included a detailed ***Senior Year Financial Aid Checklist*** in the Appendix section of this book. In addition, we have included our ***College OPTIONS Award Letter tool*** in the Appendix section. The **Award Letter Tool** will be invaluable to help you and your child to compare award letter offers from various colleges and universities, and will be an excellent tool for you and your child's next and final step—the college decision making process.

Chapter 11

Deciding on the Best Fit

"It is in your moments of decision that your destiny is shaped."
—Tony Robbins, Author and Life Coach Specialist

Now that your child has applied to several colleges and submitted the correct financial aid forms, life becomes a bit of a waiting game. The waiting time for admissions and financial aid decisions can seem terribly long. Most college admissions applications are due by November or December, yet admissions decisions and financial aid offers will not arrive in your child's e-mail inbox until sometime between March or April of his senior year. Once the admissions decisions and financial aid offers DO finally start arriving, how do you help your child decide which college will be the best fit for him?

DETERMINING THE BEST FIT FOR YOUR CHILD

First of all, when college admissions decisions arrive in the spring, do not panic if your child does not receive an admissions offer from his first choice college. California colleges and universities are becoming extremely competitive, and tens of thousands of students are denied admission to their first-choice college every year. Refer back to Chapter 6 about the California community college system. California residents are incredibly fortunate to have two pathways for students to enter into four-year institutions. The community college transfer pathway has multiple academic and financial benefits for your child and your family, so encourage your child to consider that option.

"I want to go out of town so that I can become a fully independent person, but near enough so that I can bring my laundry home."

If your child is fortunate to receive more than one offer of admission to a four-year college, congratulations! However, his hard work is not over yet. For many four-year colleges in California, May 1 is the deadline for students to notify each college regarding their fall enrollment decision. For the UC and CSU systems, incoming freshman students need to return a "Statement of Intent to Register" (SIR) by May 1, along with a deposit to hold their place in the incoming fall freshmen class. As a parent, you have done your homework, researched the colleges, reviewed the offers of financial aid, and now you and your child need to make a decision. How hard can that be? VERY hard in some cases.

HOW DO YOU HELP YOUR CHILD WITH THIS IMPORTANT LIFE DECISION?

Making this important college enrollment decision can be a very stressful time for both students and parents. As a parent, your first step should be to consult each college's website. Second, you should explore the Department of Education's "College Navigator" website at http://nces.ed.gov/collegenavigator. This site is an invaluable tool that will provide detailed information about each of the colleges you and your child are considering for enrollment, and will give you information on the important factors to consider when making your final choice.

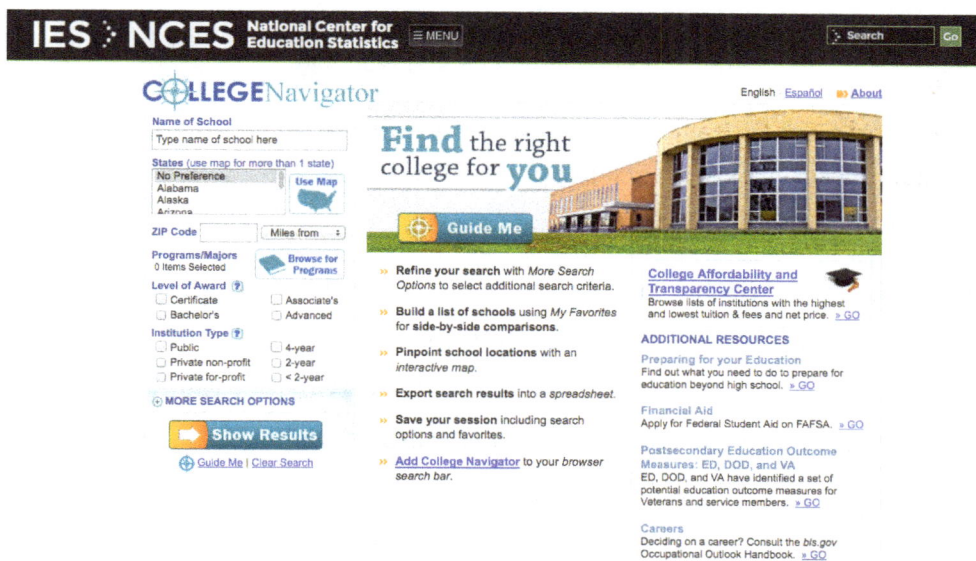

Figure 23   College Navigator Website

The Three Important Factors to Research and Consider When Deciding Which College Is the Best Fit for Your Child

1. College location, size, and campus life

College location, size, and campus life are critical factors to research during your child's decision-making process. The best way to discover this information firsthand is to personally visit the colleges. Many campuses have "College Preview Days" designed to provide students and their families with detailed information about their academic programs, student life, extracurricular activities, and the surrounding community. If your family cannot attend a formal preview day, many campuses offer daily walking tours and presentations for the general community. Refer to the college's website for information regarding incoming freshmen campus visit schedules, orientations, and campus tours.

While considering the factors of college location and size, remember that there are students who want to stay close to their families and others who would like the opportunity to go away to school to live on their own. Consider these questions:

- Does your child want to go to school in a big city or a small town?

- Does he want a small, intimate setting or a school that is big enough to be a city by itself?

- Maybe he prefers something in-between? Keep in mind that the location of a school and your child's housing options can also greatly impact the overall cost of his college education.

Questions to Ask on a College Campus Visit

If your family has the chance to visit the colleges your child is considering for enrollment in the fall, be sure to ask the following questions on your visit:

What academic services and social opportunities are available to help first-year students get settled during their first year?

- How large are the freshmen classes?
- How easy is it for students to meet with faculty?
- How difficult is it for students to register for the classes they want?
- What is the total cost of attending this college?
- What types of financial aid does this college offer?
- Are all freshmen assigned to an academic advisor?
- Where do most freshmen live?
- Does the campus tour include a tour of the dorms and dining halls?
- What kind of campus security is in place?
- Who teaches the courses for first-year students? Faculty or graduate students?
- How successful are your college graduates in finding jobs?
- What services (such as transportation and shopping) are available locally?
- What is there to do on weekends? Do most students stay or leave campus on weekends?

Research Your Questions If a Visit Is Not Possible

If you and your child are not able to visit the college before you need to decide on fall enrollment, create a list of questions you have about the campus and then contact the campus by phone or e-mail. Often, you can find contact information through department links on the college's website. You should check the college's website to see if there is a specific link for parents. Typically, the parent link will answer several of your questions and may even have a parent FAQ (Frequently Asked Questions) section. There are always links for "prospective" or "future students." Again, read the FAQs to see if they answer your questions. Contact the college directly if you find that you and your child still have unanswered questions. If your child is trying to learn more about his academic major, have him contact that department via phone or e-mail. Ask if there is a current student who might be willing to speak with him about his or her experiences. Finally, check to see if the college offers "virtual tours" of its campus online.

2. College Cost of Attendance (COA) vs. Financial Aid offered

As we discussed in Chapter 10, college cost is one of the most important factors in choosing a potential college for your child, and costs can vary significantly from school to school. While the cost of college includes tuition and fees, it also includes books, transportation, housing, and much more.

As a parent, you will want to make sure that the cost of the college is reasonable compared to your child's earning potential in his future career. In other words, you want to make sure that your child can earn enough money to cover any student loan payments he may need to make, along with living expenses, after he graduates.

Any school that distributes federal student aid is required to provide accurate information on the cost of attendance and to offer a net price calculator on its college website. This calculator will give you an idea of how much a college may cost after subtracting any financial aid offers. The average net price to attend the college is determined by subtracting the amount of financial aid from the total cost of attendance for the college or university. Another useful tool that will help you research the cost and determine the value of a college is The College Scorecard. This informative website can also be accessed at: http://www.whitehouse.gov/issues/education/higher-education/college-score-card.

This site will provide unbiased information about specific college costs, graduation rates, loan default rates, median loan borrowing amounts, and employment rates after graduation.

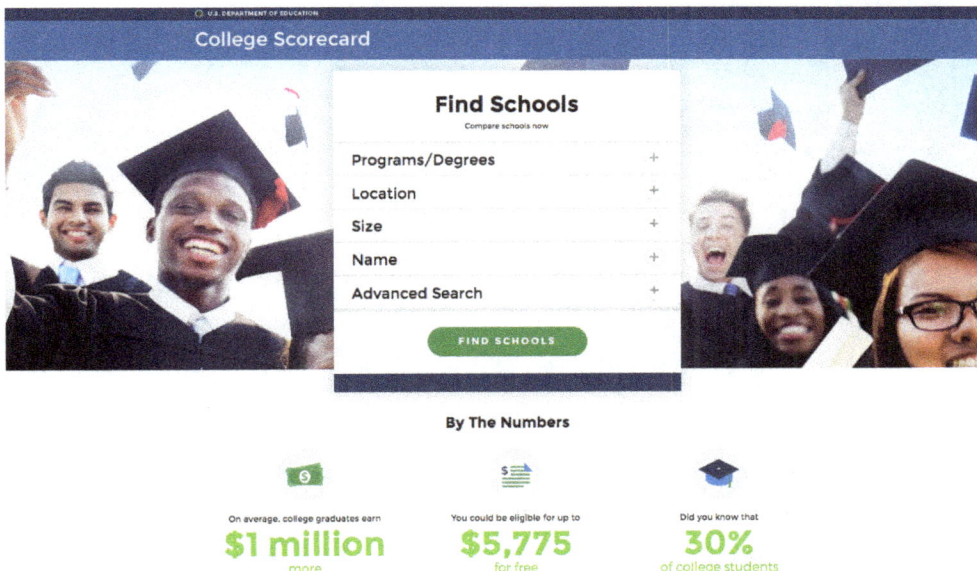

Figure 24   College Scorecard

FINANCIAL AID AWARD (OFFER) LETTERS

Financial aid award letters from each college should arrive in your child's e-mail inbox by the spring of your child's senior year. Award letters can vary greatly from college to college, so it is important to examine each one of them closely, and contact each college separately if you have any questions about its offer. Sample financial aid award letters were outlined and explained in Chapter 10. After reviewing each of your child's offers for financial aid, turn to a very useful budgeting tool from the U.S. Department of Education and which can help you compare college expenses against your family's available income, plus each college's official award of financial aid. This tool can help inform you about whether your family income plus financial aid will be able to cover all college costs for your child, and can help you see what additional savings or other support may be needed. This useful college budgeting site can be found at: https://studentaid.ed.gov/sa/prepare-for-college/budgeting.

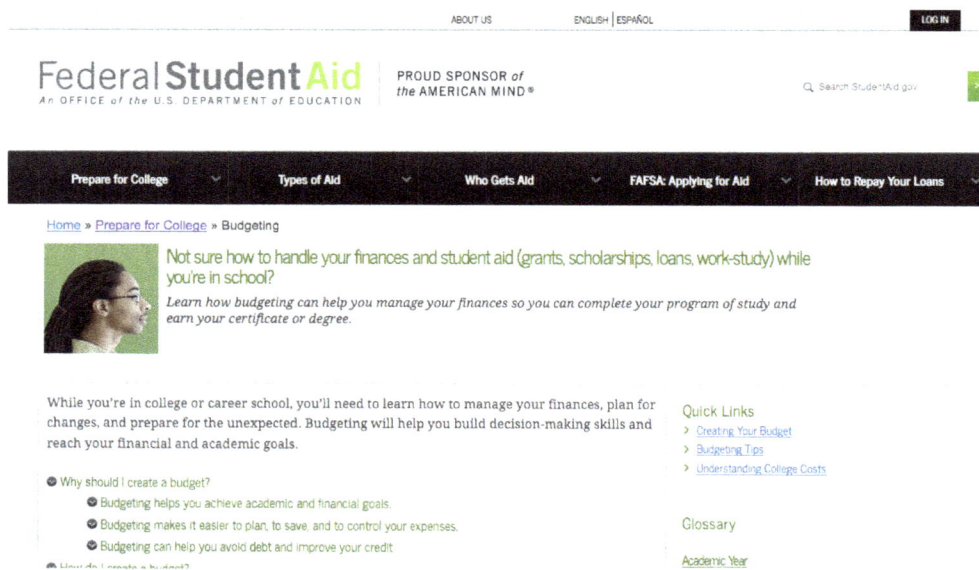

Figure 25   Budgeting Tool for College Expenses

Student Employment Assistance and Availability

If the college's offer for financial aid does not cover the entire cost of the college, your child might need to work part-time while in school. Check the college's website or speak to the financial aid staff at the college to inquire about your child's employment options. Be prepared to ask the college if it has the resources to offer student employment other than work-study. Ask important questions such as: Will the college allow your child to enroll part-time if needed? Will part-time enrollment affect his financial aid award? Does the college offer summer courses in order to reduce the length of time and money spent on completing his degree?

Second-Year Financial Aid Awards

It is also *extremely important* for parents to note that students often receive the best financial aid awards for their freshman year of college. Financial aid awards may decline drastically after the student's first year. There are several reasons why this happens. While in high school, students receive daily support from counselors and teachers who encourage them to complete the appropriate paperwork for college financial aid, including the FAFSA and scholarship applications. Once enrolled in their first year of college, the students do not have this level of support and often forget or miss critical financial aid deadlines. These missed deadlines often leave students without enough financial aid to afford their second year, and many unfortunately have to return home and enroll in a community college to continue their education. Another reason is that there is typically less scholarship money available for second-year students than there is for incoming freshmen.

3.   College outcome data

Your child's college education will most likely be one of your family's most important financial investments. Given this fact, it is critically important to achieve the best return on your investment. It is important to research how successful each college campus is in terms of retaining students from year to year, graduating students on time, the number of students who default on their student loans, the college's accreditation status and job placement rate. Thankfully, there is a "one-stop shopping resource" for parents to discover this important information. As noted earlier, the College Navigator site from the U.S. Department of Education provides this information and much more for every college institution in the nation. This site can be found at http://nces.ed.gov/collegenavigator. This useful site will provide information on the following critical factors:

- Retention rate
- Graduation rate
- Accreditation information
- Job placement rate

Retention Rate

Retention rate refers to the percentage of a college's first-year students who continue at that same college the next year. For example, a student who studies full-time in the fall semester and continues to be enrolled in that college the next fall semester is counted in this rate. Unfortunately, many first-year college students do not make it back for their sophomore year, thus costing their family money, time, and heartache. The reasons for students not returning to college are numerous, ranging from family problems, loneliness, academic struggles, and a lack of money. You do not want this to happen to your child. You and your child should look into the available campus resources and supportive services for him during his first year in college; he must then take full advantage of these resources. Colleges with strong resources for its first- and second-year students often have a very high retention rate.

Graduation Rate

As stated earlier in this chapter, your child's college education will most likely be one of your family's most important financial investments. Therefore it is vital that you determine if your first choice college will complete what it promises to deliver—to graduate your student in four years, prepared to enter the workforce or enroll into graduate school. You and your child need to know how successful each college campus is in terms of retaining students from year to year and graduating students on time.

A college's graduation rate is calculated using the percentage of a college's first-year students who complete their degree within four to six years of starting. For example, for a four-year degree program, entering students who complete within six years are counted as on-time graduates.

Accreditation

An independent agency evaluates each college, ensures that it is meeting all academic standards, and provides official accreditation documentation to the public. The College Navigator site discussed earlier will provide you with this important accreditation information.

Job Placement Rate

The "job placement rate" is the percentage of graduates who are placed, within a certain time frame, into jobs relevant to their course of study. You may have to do a little research to locate this rate, but the best place to check is the college's website. You may also want to contact the college's career center to find out what kind of job placement services it offers to current students and graduates. If the college is a career/technical school, ask your local employers what they think about the college. Finally, ask to speak to recent graduates about their experience at the college and about their ability to find related work after completing their degree.

MAKING THE FINAL COLLEGE ENROLLMENT DECISION— A HELPFUL DECISION TOOL

Finally, we'll look at a sample decision-making tool that can be used by you and your child to help with the college selection process. In the Appendix section of this book, you will find a blank copy of this decision-making tool for you and your child *to both* customize separately. The instructions for using this decision-making tool follows.

Step one: Select your top eight college selection FACTORS

You and your child should create separate lists of the top eight factors you are looking for in a college. As expected, these lists will probably differ. While your student may be interested in factors such as the dorms, the recreation center, and/or social atmosphere, you may be more concerned with items such as freshmen retention rate, safety statistics, and affordability. What is most important about this phase of the decision-making process is to be honest with each other about your top factors and really listen to each other about which ones are most important to each of you, and why.

Examples of factors from which to choose include: Major or interest area

- Even if your child is undecided, he will most likely have some idea of a major or career interest.
- Does the college have a policy on changing majors, and is it relatively easy or difficult?

Geography/location

- Does your child prefer year-round sunshine or a more diverse climate?
- Does he want to study abroad or from the comforts of home?

Rural or urban setting

- Is a larger school in a big city more preferable to a smaller school in a rural town?
- Does your child wish to live in a college-town where basically the area caters to the college/university or a more removed setting with less focus on college life?
- How much change does your child want from where he lives now?

Size of student population

- Is your child interested in a larger college with 30,000 students or a smaller college with an enrollment of 1,500?

- Larger schools typically have extensive campuses with a variety of services and activities.

- Smaller colleges may be more individualized and offer a more personal experience.

- Student/teacher ratios should be considered.

Type of college/university

- Is the school public or private?

- Does it have a religious affiliation? Is the college single sex or coed?

- Does the college specialize in one particular area or does it provide a broader education?

Costs, scholarships, and financial aid

- Public schools are typically less expensive than private or out-of-state schools.

- Private colleges often have more endowments and can offer more scholarships.

- When comparing college costs, make sure you take all things into consideration, such as tuition, room and board, textbooks, etc.

Step two: Assign a weight to each of your top eight factors

Once you have placed your eight factors in the top boxes of this tool, assign a weight or value to those factors using a scale of 1 to 10, with 10 being the most important.

Step three: Assign a score to each factor

The final step is to score each factor, from 1 to 10. Then, multiply the score by that factor's weight to find the "rating points" for that factor. Total the rating points for each college campus and write the total in the far right column. A sample tool showing completed ratings is shown in Figure 26.

The best part about this unique tool is that it is completely customizable. You and your child are both able to choose the factors that are most important to each of you. After you each complete this exercise, it will then be time to sit down and have a very honest discussion with your child about which college choice scored the highest for both of you, and which choice will be the overall best fit for your entire family.

college OPTIONS

Decision Tool	Individual Campus Factors to Consider (factors that matter to YOU)	Reputation of Academics/ Accreditation	Majors that interest you	Cost	Size of campus (does it "fit" you?)	Social Activities/ Environment	Availability of Housing (Dorms, Apartments)	Sports (playing or attending events)	Distance from home	Note: Each factor is created by you.
	Assign a weight to that factor (between 1-10)	10	10	10	8	6	6	5	3	Total Rating Points
	Name of college: College #1									
	Score:	8	3	5	8	3	5	3	2	
	Rating Points:	80	30	50	64	18	30	15	6	293
Campuses being considered.	Name of college: College #2									
	Score:	6	8	6	6	6	9	8	3	
For each campus, assign a score to each factor.	Rating Points:	60	80	60	48	36	54	40	9	387
	Name of college:									
	Score:									
Mulitply the score by that factor's weight to find the "rating points" for that factor.	Rating Points:									
	Name of college:									
	Score:									
	Rating Points:									
Total the rating points for that campus and write the total in the far right column.	Name of college:									
	Score:									
	Rating Points:									
	Name of college:									
	Score:									
	Rating Points:									
	Name of college:									
	Score:									
	Rating Points:									

Figure 26   Sample College Decision-Making Tool.
Copyright © 2016 by College OPTIONS. Reprinted by permission.

Keep in mind, making a college enrollment choice is NOT an easy decision, and it may take some time and tears to get through it. That is perfectly normal and to be expected. Take comfort from the words of an experienced mom who has been there, done that:

Advice from a real mom about the college enrollment decision-making process:

"I remember how stressed I felt when my oldest son and our family were trying to decide on where he would attend college. My heart wanted to find a way to send him to his dream school, but my head knew I couldn't mortgage our future to do this. I also felt we had to keep in mind that we would be setting a precedence for our other three children who planned to attend a college or university. Our family had to take a realistic look at what portion of the family budget could be diverted towards our son's education and what income he might be able to contribute through his summer jobs and working part-time during the school year. We examined the cost of attendance at each potential college. Our son applied for financial aid and scholarships and we waited to see what money would be offered by each college and awarded in scholarship money. Once we received the financial aid offers from each college, we knew which schools were realistic choices."

Chapter 12

The First-Year College Student

"You are never strong enough that you don't need help."
—Cesar Chavez

Congratulations! You and your child have worked extremely hard to prepare for college and it's now finally time to realize the benefits of all that hard work. Although your child is now over eighteen years of age, she will still need your assistance and support, only in different ways. This transition in parenting can be as hard for the parent as it is for the child enrolling in college for the first time. In a few short months, your child will soon embark on her college journey. Whether she enrolls in a local college or university, or attends one away from home, your lives are bound to change in several ways.

WHAT TO EXPECT—LIVING AT HOME, ATTENDING A LOCAL COLLEGE/UNIVERSITY

Everyone associates the college experience with dorm life but the truth is, not everyone lives on campus. If your child is going to a community college or a commuter university close to home, chances are she's going to be rooming with Mom and Dad—and there's going to be an adjustment period for both of you. There are other options, of course, but the majority of community college kids live at home or in an apartment.

Freshman Ryan Brenneman was having a tough
time acclimating to life away from home.

"Pros" of a Student Living at Home

Starting college is a major rite of passage, one that is both exciting and anxiety-producing. So on the upside, your child gets to go through that process from the comfort of home, where the food is vastly better than the dining commons, and the bathroom is shared by just a few people, not fifty. There are definite benefits for parents, too. Your food bill may stay high, but you will still save thousands of dollars a year on room and board bills. You'll have the company of a bright, interesting student living in your home, and you won't have to worry about the empty nest blues.

"Cons" of a Student Living at Home

Your new college student living at home can have its difficulties as well. It is sometimes hard for commuter students to make new friends and settle into college life without a dormitory's sense of instant community.

The following tips might help to smooth that transition for both you and your college student who is continuing to live under your roof:

- Naturally, college students living in the dorms enjoy considerably more freedom than high school students; of course, some college students living at home would like these same freedoms. To smooth out possible differences of opinion in this area, start by sitting down and talking through the major issues—such things as privacy, telephone and computer time, use of the car, and curfews.

- Encourage your child to update her room and bring home some college "swag" to hang on the walls.

- In order to fully integrate herself into campus life, encourage your child to study on campus, at the library, in the quad or campus coffeehouse, or wherever other students congregate.

- Make her college's orientation session mandatory. If there is a parent session, plan to go as well. Your presence sends your child a critical message that her college education is important to you.

- Encourage her to get involved in extracurricular activities on campus by joining clubs or intramural sports teams.

Be prepared to see less of your child, especially during the summer after her senior year. The closer it gets to college departure time, the less you can expect to see of your child as she will likely be spending every waking hour with her friends, who also might be leaving their hometown very soon. Allow your child and her friends this special time together. Try to not be hurt by your child's need to bond with friends whose lives will all change forever in just a few short weeks.

What to Expect—Attending a College/University Away from Home

If at all possible, if your child is going to enroll in college away from home, encourage her to submit an application to live on campus in the dorms. Not every college makes dorm housing available, and living on campus does not fit into every family's budget. But for those who can take advantage of this option, it allows new students to more easily become involved in the social and academic life of the campus. Late-night hanging out in the dorm, going to games or performances, and the chance to visit TAs (Teaching Assistants) and professors whenever they are available are just some of the many benefits of on-campus life. One large study found that: "Students who live on campus generally interact more with faculty and peers and are more satisfied with their undergraduate experience." (Source: National Center for Education Statistics, http://nces.ed.gov).

The Empty Nest Syndrome

The time period before your child leaves home for college can be a difficult time for both the parent and the child who is leaving. It can be hard to let go after seventeen or eighteen years of parenting. Following are a few suggestions to help prepare you for the challenges of the transition ahead.

Now that the last child had finally left for college, Dot and Neville went through the usual 'empty nest' grieving process

Remember That This Is a Time of Conflicting Emotions for Both Parents and Child

As a parent you may be excited about the opportunities awaiting your child, but also experience a sense of loss. It will help to talk with other parents who are going through the same process, as they will also most likely be experiencing the same conflicting emotions.

Remember That Your Child Is Having These Same Feelings

At this crossroad of her life, your child is also being pulled between her past and future. She is most likely experiencing a wide range of emotions, too. Your child might be moodier than normal, a typical sign of the ups and downs of her feelings during this transitional time. Remember that even positive emotions are normal.

While you may feel loss and wish again for the "early years" of your child's life, at the same time you may be looking forward to more peace and quiet at home or to spending more time with other family members. All of these reactions are normal.

Do Not Ignore Your Feelings

Do not ignore how you are affected by the transition of your child going away to college. A healthy approach is to talk about your feelings with family and friends.

Acknowledge the Importance of This Milestone

You have successfully guided your child to become a productive member of society. Now, it is time that she practices all that you have taught her. By providing your child with an opportunity to go to college, you have given her a priceless gift. Find an outlet for yourself.

When your child enters this stage of life, it is normal for her to become active in a life separate from the family. Do not take it personally when she does not have the same amount of time for you as before. Consider taking up activities that provide new challenges that can help you re-channel the energies previously spent on your child.

THINGS TO DO AND NOT TO DO THE SUMMER BEFORE YOUR CHILD STARTS COLLEGE

Talk about Your Family's Financial Strategies before the School Year Starts

After carefully reviewing the financial aid award offer at the college your child will attend, develop a financial budget and strategy about who will pay for what expenses. For example, some parents agree to pay for books and supplies, while their child is responsible for costs associated with snacks, movies, and entertainment. Reinforce the importance of responsible use of credit and debit cards. It is critical that your child set up her own bank account and learn how to balance a checkbook, use an ATM, and responsibly handle a debit card. There are numerous money management apps for smartphones and online resources. One of the best is http://www.mint.com.

Talk about Your Child's Academic Goals and Expectations Ahead of Time

Many college freshmen do not do as well academically their first quarter or semester as they did while in high school. This is extremely normal. This fact may also cause your child to change her mind about her major or chosen field of study. Before the school year begins, ask her what she hopes to accomplish during her first year, and have a heart-to-heart talk about the academic and social differences between high school and college. For example, professors do not take class attendance, and students also end up with a great amount of unstructured free time. This free time should be spent on studying. Unfortunately, many first-year students are experiencing new freedom and do not discover the importance of studying during free time until it is too late.

Talk to Your Child about How You Want to Stay in Touch

Do you want a scheduled day and time to talk with your child or do you prefer to be more spontaneous? A cell phone can be a wonderful way to keep in touch or it can be, as one student described, an "electronic leash." Encourage your child to use her phone as little as possible, as it can be an immediate and problematic time zapper. E-mail and text messaging are wonderful ways to keep in touch; however, you should not count on a reply to every message.

Do Not Try to Solve Your Child's Problems

During your child's first year of college, you are likely to hear about all of the problems and issues she is facing rather than the good news. College students usually call, e-mail, or text their parents for reassurance when things are not going well, yet they will most likely contact their friends with the latest exciting news. When you get those late-night texts or calls (and you will) you can encourage your child to use the appropriate campus resources such as going to health services or speaking with a resident advisor, academic advisor, etc.

Talk about Future Changes at Home

Keep your child informed about any major changes taking place in the future at home. College students want parents to accept all the changes they are making in their lives, yet they want everything to remain the same at home. It is important to keep your child informed about changes at home, whether it is about moving a younger sibling into her room, an illness in the family, or the death of a pet. Your child needs this information from you in order to feel secure as a member of the family while she is away at school.

YOUR CHILD'S FIRST YEAR IN COLLEGE—12 PARENTING TIPS

You want to do everything you can as a parent to ensure that your child not only enters college, but most importantly, completes her college degree. It is a harsh reality, but very important for you to know, that only six out of every ten students nationwide who begin college actually complete their degree within six years (http://www.completecollege.org). Research shows that a student's first few weeks on campus are the most critical in determining whether or not they will persist to complete a degree at that campus (Levitz and Noel 1989). The transition from high school to college can be very difficult for students, and parental support is critical to help students ease through the transition.

Whether your child is staying home to attend the local community or four-year college, or moving away from home to do so, the following parents tips still apply:

1. Expect her to change—but not too much

Your child will change. It is natural, inevitable, and it can be inspiring and beautiful. College, and the experiences associated with it, can affect changes in social, vocational, and personal behavior. An up-to-now shy child may blossom to become a sorority member, pre-med student, or campus leader. Remember that your child will be basically the same person you sent away to college, aside from natural changes in interest and personality. Do not expect too much, too soon. Maturation is not an instantaneous or overnight process, so be patient.

2. Encourage your child to seek out new experiences

It is not all about grades. Your child also needs to experience working, internships, and extracurricular activities. These activities will allow her to build her résumé, relationships, and workplace skills ranging from time management and customer service to leadership. Connections made through a part-time job or an internship can lead your child to her first job after college and/or provide letters of recommendation for employment or graduate school. Ask her if she has visited the career office on campus by the end of her freshman year and encourage her to find out about summer internships. Throughout high school your child most likely had a part-time job and/or engaged in some form of sport or activity. This participation should continue while she is in college. Ask your child how she plans to stay involved in the things she enjoyed doing before starting college.

3. Discuss the consequences of excessive drinking and drug use

Many college students experiment with campus drinking, recreational drugs, and too much partying. First-year college students can quickly get in over their heads and wind up in all sorts of trouble—to themselves and to others. Educate your child about the importance of acting responsibly—even when her fellow college students do not. It is important to have an open and calm discussion before college starts. Believe it or not, these conversations will help limit and decrease the amount of experimentation your child does in this arena.

4.   Allow her to grow by handling small conflicts on her own

Demonstrate to your child that you have confidence in her to handle the small bumps in the road. For example, if she is having drama with an unhappy roommate, suggest that she first address her concerns with that person; and then suggest involving a resident advisor. Do not just jump in and immediately demand that a room switch must be made.

5.   Communicate with her—even if she does not communicate back right away

Although new students are typically eager to experience all the "away-from-home" independence they can fit in those first weeks, most are still anxious for family ties and the security those ties bring. This surge of independence may be misinterpreted by some sensitive parents as rejection, but most new students (although most would not admit it) would give anything for some news of home and family, however mundane it may seem to you. There is nothing more depressing than a week of not hearing from anyone back home. So go ahead and write or text your child. Although she may not answer you (the "you-write-one and they-write-one rule" does not always seem to apply to college students), your child will appreciate your thoughtfulness. Texts and e-mails are better than phone calls because they can be read and re-read at especially lonely moments. Keep communication current and open, but try not to become a "helicopter parent." Many well-meaning parents want to track their child's every movement at college. Resist the temptation to call or text five times a day. Let your child develop a sense of independence and personal responsibility.

6.   Do not worry about sad calls, texts, or e-mails

Parenting can be a thankless job, especially during the first year of college. Often, troubles become too much for a new college student to handle and the only place to turn to is home. Unfortunately, this is often the only time that the urge to communicate is felt so strongly, so you never hear about the "A" paper, the new significant other, or the roommate relationship triumph. In these "crisis times" your son or daughter can unload troubles or tears and, after the drama has passed, return to routine, while you inherit the burden of worry. Be patient with these "emergency" calls or texts, and know that they too, will soon pass.

7.   Visit your child—but not too often

Visits by parents—especially when accompanied by shopping sprees and/or dinners out—are another part of first-year events that new college students are reluctant to admit liking but appreciate greatly. Faked dislike of these visits is just another part of the new college student experience. These visits give both the student and their parents the opportunity to learn more about the new things that both are experiencing. However, spur of the moment "surprise" visits are usually NOT appreciated. Prior scheduling of visits is very important recognition that your child has responsibilities and plans that she may not be able to or want to change at the last minute.

8. Encourage your child to ask questions in class, seek help, and use the campus resources—they are there for a reason!

Silence is not golden in college. Asking for help or support is a sign of your child's interest, engagement, and strength. Faculty members and advisors on campus value students who are curious and who politely advocate for themselves.

Furthermore, campus resources are funded by tuition dollars. Not to use every resource is a waste of your tuition dollars. If your child is struggling to write a paper or has not done well on an exam, then ask if she has been to the campus writing center or met with her professors or has asked for tutoring. Remind her that it is better to get guidance than muddle along alone. Stay calm if poor grades happen—it is normal.

9. Try not to worry too much about your child's grades

Grades present another potential point of stress between parents and students. Due to federal privacy laws, colleges and universities will not allow parent access to student information. Only your child will be allowed to decide whether her academic records—course schedules and grades—will be shared with you. Remember, your child has specific rights to academic privacy. However, you may feel that if you are helping to finance your child's education, then you also have the right to remain informed about your investment. Discuss this issue with your child before the academic year begins, with the goal of agreeing on a plan for keeping you informed of her academic progress.

Parents and children both may get a shock when grades first come out after midterm exams. For students who have always excelled in school and parents with great expectations, a C, or for that matter, even a B, can be traumatic. Parents should assure themselves—and one another—that grades earned are not a final judgment on the abilities of the student or on her professional career prospects.

10. Never, ever, call a professor, department chair, or dean

Unlike middle and high school, there are no parent-teacher conferences in college. Professors do not want to hear from parents. At some colleges, there is even an unofficial "Dean of Parents" whose primary job is to help parents understand their new and different role in their child's education. Your child is now on their own on a college campus, pursuing his or her own future. Try not to get in the way.

11. Protect the last two weeks of your child's quarter or semester

In many college courses, up to 70 percent of the course grade is based on an exam or project in the last two weeks of the term. Do not distract your child with winter vacation plans, worries about finances or what to major in, family events and celebrations, or other activities during this crucial end-of-term time frame. These are "make-or-break" times for your child. Respect them.

12. Know when to get involved

It is time for the parent to get involved when the tearful calls/texts/e-mails outnumber the happy ones or when other behaviors arise, such as frequent illnesses, excessive fatigue, negative changes in behavior or appearance, or talk of hopelessness or lack of purpose. At that point, call the college immediately to alert them to the problem. A great deal of help and assistance will be available to both you and your child.

FIRST-GENERATION COLLEGE STUDENTS

First-generation college students are those students whose parent(s) have not earned a college degree. These students may enter college with very limited knowledge about the jargon, traditions, and patterns of expected behavior associated with college enrollment. These factors may prevent first-generation college students from fully engaging in a college setting and may contribute to their early departure before the completion of their degree. No matter how intelligent and capable they are, first-generation college students may benefit from additional support as they adjust to a new environment. If you are a parent of a first-generation college student, it can be helpful to learn more about what other first-generation college students have experienced, as well as what can be done to help maximize your child's performance and experience as she works toward attaining her degree. How are first-generation college students' experiences different?

First-generation college students tend to come from working-class families from various cultural and ethnic backgrounds. First-generation college students may start at a community college, attend college part-time, live off-campus or with family or relatives, delay entering college after high-school graduation, or work full-time while they are enrolled in college. While certainly immersed in an exciting experience, some first-generation college students receive limited support from their families while attending college. Their families may not understand the demands of a college schedule and the academic rigor that goes along with it. These students may also feel the added responsibility from their families to be "the one" who succeeds in college. Despite having good academic performance in high school, first-generation college students are also susceptible to doubts about their academic and motivational abilities and may believe that they are not college material. Because of these numerous obstacles, and because they may have to manage the demands of family and different cultures of home and college, first-generation college students may find it difficult to feel part of the college socially and academically. Fortunately, there are things these students can do to gain confidence and feel more comfortable.

If you are a parent of a first-generation college student, you should first know that she will not be alone. Many of the feelings she will experience are normal and to be expected. First-generation college students often experience a range of feelings about being the first in their family to attend and complete college.

What are some common feelings for first-generation students?

Excitement and Anxiety—Many students are thrilled but also somewhat frightened about being away from home at college, living on their own, and being the first in the family to attend college. These students may ask themselves, "Am I cut out to be a college student?" despite their strong academic performance in high school.

Responsibility—Many first-generation students have to help pay for their education, perhaps more so than students of higher socioeconomic backgrounds. In addition to their financial responsibility, these students may be pressured by family and friends to return home often, and may receive mixed messages about their changing identities (for example, students wanting to succeed, but not wanting to be different from the rest of the family or their peers).

Pride—These students often feel an overwhelming sense of pride about being the first in their families to attend and complete college. A college degree can provide many opportunities. This is an important accomplishment!

Guilt—In addition to pride, many first-generation college students may feel guilt about having the opportunity to attend college while others in the family did not have that opportunity. These students may wonder if it is fair for them to be at school while their parents struggle financially at home. They may feel the need to go home to help support their families. First-generation college students may also feel guilty about their academic performance if it is not as good as they or their families would like.

Embarrassment and Shame—These students may feel embarrassment over their socio-economic status or the level of education in their family. First-generation college students may try to act like their family is more highly educated or financially advantaged than they really are. There may be embarrassment around being different from their peers at college, particularly if their peers have had multiple generations of family members attend college or if they seem to know the 'lingo' when a first-generation student may not.

Confusion—First-generation college students may feel 'out of the loop' when it comes to college processes and procedures such as application, graduation, job or graduate school searches, etc. They may not be aware of the resources available to them or of options available to them after graduation.

RECOMMENDATIONS FOR PARENTS OF FIRST-GENERATION COLLEGE STUDENTS

Most first-generation college students who drop out of college are likely to do so within the first one or two years. What can you do to ensure that your child completes her degree and has a positive college experience?

Find Support

First-generation college students are more likely to live off-campus, work while taking classes, and be enrolled part-time than their non–first-generation classmates. By becoming involved on campus, your child may receive the support she needs and begin to feel more integrated with other college students. Encourage her to apply for and participate in any Summer Bridge Program that is offered. Summer Bridge Programs offer college preparation and orientation programs and often house students in a residential setting on college campuses for two to six weeks before the fall term begins.

Encourage her to join groups, organizations, or support groups that are of interest to her. Also, encourage her to talk with people she trusts, perhaps her families and friends, about what she is experiencing as she adjusts to college and a new environment.

Encourage Communication about What She Is Experiencing

In times of transition, it can be helpful for students to communicate what they are experiencing and what they need from one another. As your child grows and develops, she may begin to feel different from her family and peers. This is a natural process for all college students, and it can be helpful to share her experiences with others.

Utilize Resources

Urge your child to take advantage of mentoring programs as well as the variety of offices and programs designed to assist her. Many colleges and universities have specific programs for first-generation college students to provide advising, tutoring, financial aid counseling, and much more. These services can help your child navigate the college terrain as well as feel understood and connected. She can also benefit from getting to know an upper-level student who can show her the ropes. Finding a first-generation college student mentor who has already been in college for a few years can be especially helpful, as that student can share tips on how to deal with the first year of college. Some of the programs providing academic resources and summer orientation bridge programs for first-generation college students include the Extended Opportunity Programs & Services (EOPS) program at community colleges, the Educational Opportunity Program (EOP) program at the CSU and UC systems, and the TRIO Student Support Services (SSS) programs at both two- and four-year colleges and universities. Encourage your child to look into each of these programs on campus.

Encourage Balance

Your child has a lot to juggle! With the demands of academics, work, family, and a social life, it is important that your child finds a way to balance competing needs. Time management is essential, and having a schedule can help her manage those competing interests and demands. Remember that the perseverance, resilience, resourcefulness, and hard work that helped her get into college will also help keep her there.

Learn about the College Process and What to Expect

It can be helpful for family members to attend orientations, meet with advisors, and get to know the campus resources so they can be more familiar with what the student is experiencing.

INDICATORS OF DIFFICULTY WITH COLLEGE ADJUSTMENT

No matter how near or far away adolescents attend college, parents generally stay connected and want to ensure their children's well-being and safety. It is important that parents stay in touch with their college students and be aware of signs of difficulty adjusting to college life and of potential stressors related to this very important transition. Possible indicators of distress and difficulties with college include:

- An expressed need for help
- Prolonged sadness or depressed mood
- Tearfulness, crying, and frequent emotional outbursts
- Excessive irritability, hostility, anger, or resentment
- Loss of interest and pleasure in activities once enjoyed
- Withdrawal from social interactions
- Statements of loneliness
- Difficulty developing a social network on campus
- Loss of energy and fatigue
- Agitation and restlessness
- Changes in sleep patterns
- Trouble concentrating or making decisions
- Missing class often
- Falling behind in schoolwork or failing classes
- Substantial changes in appetite, eating patterns, or weight
- Feeling of guilt, hopelessness, or worthlessness
- Risk-taking behaviors, such as unprotected sex
- Excessive use of alcohol or drugs
- Hopelessness
- Thoughts or statements of death or suicide

Speak to your child if you see any significant changes in emotions, behaviors, or social activities. If you notice a number of the risk indicators in your college student, you and your child are encouraged to seek professional help. You can also encourage your college student to speak to counselors at the university counseling center.

MOST IMPORTANT PARENTING TIP OF ALL—BE PATIENT AND CARING

College is a learning process for everyone involved. Remember, you are ALL going through this for the first time. There is a learning curve, and it is important for you and your child to be patient with yourselves and each other. Prepare to be sympathetic, supportive, and patient. Recognize that doing nothing is often the best option. The fact is that after a few wobbly weeks or months, most first-year college students settle in quite nicely. Please remember that your student's maturing process—like your own—will likely involve ups and downs, academic twists and turns, intimate relationships entered into and ended. A healthy respect for your child's autonomy, good judgment, and adherence to the values you have helped instill is likely to be rewarded in the long term. Finally, show your child that you care. No matter how your child does in college, you will always be her parent, and she will always be your child. Show concern, compassion, and love throughout your child's college life. College is a demanding and emotionally challenging time. It is made easier when parents show that they care.

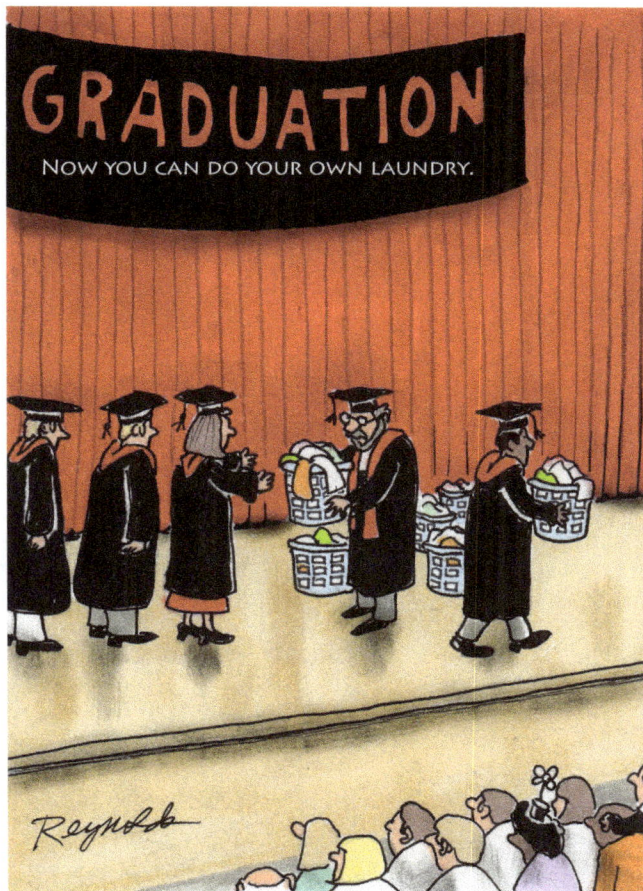

Appendix

High School Timeline

Activities for Parents

9TH GRADE

HOW CAN I LEARN ABOUT COLLEGE OPTIONS FOR MY STUDENT	
Activity	**Details**
What are the different colleges my student can attend?	Learn about all of the college options your student has. Explore the differences between public, private, and independent colleges. **Discover the four systems of higher education in California (Community College, California State University, University of California, and Independent/Private Universities).** See below for more information!
Learn about the California Community Colleges	The **California Community Colleges (CCC)** consist of 113 campuses across the state that provide programs for your student to: • Transfer to a four-year college. • Pursue career education programs (such as licenses or certifications). • Take developmental courses or enroll in "catch-up" programs. • Take classes for cultural growth, life enrichment, and skills improvement. **For more information, visit** http://www.cccco.edu/.

Continued.

Provided by: CCGI: CALIFORNIA COLLEGE GUIDANCE INITIATIVE

Activity	Details
Learn about California State Universities	The **California State Universities (CSU's)** are publicly sponsored colleges. There are 23 campuses in California that offer over 2,700 undergraduate degree and certificate programs. The 23 CSU campuses are: • California State University, Bakersfield • California State University, Channel Islands • California State University, Chico • California State University, Dominguez Hills • California State University, East Bay • California State University, Fresno • California State University, Fullerton • Humboldt State University • California State University, Long Beach • California State University, Los Angeles • California State University, Maritime Academy • California State University, Monterey Bay • California State University, Northridge • California State Polytechnic University, Pomona • California State University, Sacramento • California State University, San Bernardino • San Diego State University • San Francisco State University • San José State University • California Polytechnic State University, San Luis Obispo • California State University, San Marcos • Sonoma State University • California State University, Stanislaus **For more information, visit** http://www.calstate.edu/.
Learn about University of California (UC)	The **University of California (UC)** includes nine undergraduate campuses throughout the state and a 10th campus that offers professional and graduate programs in health sciences. The UC offers thousands of undergraduate and graduate programs to its students. The ten UC campuses are: • UCLA • UC Berkeley • UC Irvine • UC Santa Barbara • UC Merced • UC San Diego • UC Davis • UC Santa Cruz • UC Riverside • UC San Francisco (professional and graduate only) **For more information, visit** http://www.universityofcalifornia.edu/.

Activity	Details
Learn about the California private, independent colleges	**California's independent colleges and universities** are an excellent choice for many students. There are over 75 nonprofit, independent colleges and universities in the state. These colleges and universities are represented by the Association of Independent California Colleges and Universities (AICCU). **For more information, visit** http://www.aiccu.edu/.
Learn about out-of-state public and private, independent colleges	With nearly 5,000 colleges in the country, there is bound to be one for your student! Just like colleges here in California, colleges in other states come in all shapes and sizes, with schools serving less than 2,000 students, to colleges serving more than 30,000 students. **For more information on colleges throughout the country, visit** https://collegescorecard.ed.gov/.

HIGH SCHOOL PLANNING ACTIVITIES

Activity	Details
Taking the right classes	Make sure your student is taking the correct courses. It is important to understand that your student must successfully complete college preparatory classes in order to get into college. Read more below on what those college preparatory courses consist of.
What are "a-g" courses?	There are 15 "a-g" subject requirements that students must take and pass in order to be eligible for University of California (UC) or California State University (CSU). To meet "a-g" requirements, students must take: (a) 2 years of History (b) 4 years of English (c) 3 years of Mathematics (4 recommended) (d) 2 years of Laboratory Science (3 years recommended) (e) 2 years of Language other than English (3 years recommended) (f) 1 year of Visual/Performing Arts (g) 1 year of College-Preparatory Elective(s)
Exploring your student's interests	Does your student know what career fields interests him/her? Or, the job functions that are the best match for him/her? Encourage your student to take a career assessment that will help guide your student to determine which careers match his/her interests. **TIP:** Check with your student's school counselor about free career assessments that may be available for him/her to take at school.

10TH GRADE

HIGH SCHOOL PLANNING ACTIVITIES	
Activity	**Details**
Become familiar with "a-g" courses	**"a-g" courses** are college preparatory courses that your student must take to gain acceptance in to a CSU or UC campus. Your student's school has specific courses that are "a-g" approved. Be sure to ask your student's counselor the following question: "Is my student on track with his or her "a-g" requirements? "This is different than asking "Is my student on track to graduate?" because some high school graduation requirements do not always include "a-g" courses. You want your student to be on track with "a-g" so s/he qualifies to apply for universities in addition to graduating from high school.
GPA Matters: monitor your student's GPA	**GPA, or grade point average,** refers to a number assigned to the grades your student receives in his/her classes. Each grade (A, A–, B+, B, etc.) is assigned a specific number of points and then all grades are averaged to calculate students' GPAs. For example, if an A is worth 4.0 points and a student earns all A's, then their GPA is 4.0. There are two types of GPAs: • Unweighted: the average point value a student earns in all completed courses, and • Weighted: takes into account the extra points received when taking Advanced Placement (AP), International Baccalaureate (IB), and Honors courses. For example, an A in an AP, IB, or Honors course is given 5.0 points To calculate your student's GPA, you can add the points earned in all courses and divide that number by the total number of courses. **Visit** http://www.csumentor.edu/planning/high_school/gpa_calculator.asp **to access a free GPA calculator.**

FINANCIAL AID PLANNING ACTIVITIES	
Activity	**Details**
What is financial aid?	Financial aid is money that is used to help pay for college. Students who are eligible for financial aid can receive loans, grants, or scholarships, and other types of financial aid from the following sources: • Federal government • California state government • Colleges and universities • Community groups, including religious and civic organizations, professional associations, and corporations Students must apply for financial aid during their senior year of high school and every year they are in college. In most cases, parents also need to complete forms for their students to apply for financial aid. **To learn more about financial aid, visit** https://studentaid. ed.gov/sa/.
How can my student get a scholarship?	Scholarships are free money awarded based on grades, exam scores, major, or other criteria. To apply for scholarships, there are a number of requirements that might include writing essays, submitting a photo or video interview, and formal applications. Thousands of scholarships exist in the United States, and your student may qualify for both local and national scholarships. It is important for your student to research as many scholarships as possible and apply to as many as s/he qualifies for! As your student finds scholarships, make sure s/he saves and tracks them! **For more information from StudentAid.ed.gov about applying to scholarships, visit** https://studentaid.ed.gov/ types/grants-scholarships/finding-scholarships. **For more information from Big Future about applying to scholarships,** https://bigfuture.collegeboard.org/scholarship-search.

11TH GRADE

COLLEGE EXPLORATION ACTIVITIES	
Activity	**Details**
What kind of degree will my student get when they finish college?	Are there different types of degrees? Yes, your student has several options depending on what their career goals are. There are **four (4) types of degrees** your student can earn. • **Career/Technical degrees:** Career/Technical programs do not have a specific period attached to them. These programs prepare individuals for careers that don't require a bachelor's or associate's degree. Career/Technical programs often award students with licenses or certifications after successful completion. Places to complete career/technical programs are at community colleges. • **Associate's degrees:** Associate's degrees are what have historically been referred to as two-year degrees. This is because associate's programs aim at completion within two years. But students can finish these degrees in more or less time. Completion time depends on the type of program, if a student attends full-time versus part-time, and other factors. Associate's degrees can be completed at community colleges. • **Bachelor's degrees:** Bachelor's degrees are what have historically been referred to as four-year degrees. This is because bachelor's programs aim at completion within four years. Bachelor's degrees can be completed at four-year colleges and universities. • **Graduate degrees:** After earning a bachelor's degree, students can further their knowledge on a specific field of study by pursuing a higher degree in that field. This degree is known as a graduate degree, and often referred to as a professional degree. For example, if a student wishes to be a doctor, a bachelor's degree in Biology is not sufficient to be a doctor or practice as one. That student needs to attend graduate school, in this case medical school, and receive his Doctor of Medicine. It is important your student knows what career s/he wants to pursue so that they can figure out what kind of degree s/he should go to college for. Once your student knows the type of degree, it can help to narrow down which types of colleges to apply to during his/her senior year.

COLLEGE EXPLORATION ACTIVITIES	
Activity	**Details**
When should my student apply for college?	In California, the CSU and UC have a hard deadline of November 30th of the student's senior year. For more detailed information on application deadlines, check out the College Planning section of the 12th grade timeline. **CSU application opens on October 1st of their senior year and applications must be submitted by November 30th of the student's senior year. Learn more at http://www.csumentor.edu/.** **UC applications open on August 1st and applications must be submitted by November 30th of the student's senior year. Learn more at** https://admissions.universityofcalifornia.edu/.
Can my student apply for college early?	Most colleges and universities have regular admission, rolling admission, and early decision. • **Rolling Admission** typically means that the college has no application deadlines. In other words, the college accepts applications throughout the year. Because they accept students throughout the year, however, it is possible that they fill up quickly, so it is important to apply as early as possible. Aim to apply before the end of the school year! • Colleges that offer **Early Decision** plans offer earlier application deadlines. These colleges then give these students decisions on their applications sooner. If a student applies under Early Decision and gets accepted, s/he must agree to accept an offer of admission and withdraw any applications to all other schools. • There is another early application option called **Early Action** which has an earlier application deadline, like Early Decision, but students do not have to accept an offer of admission if they are accepted Early Actions. There are benefits and drawbacks to Early Decision and Early Action depending on your student's college planning needs. Talk with your student and his/her counselor to decide if Early Decision or Early Action is a good choice for him/her.
Does my student have to take a test to get in to college?	Yes, students must take an entrance exam as part of their college application. Most colleges, will require that students take one of these entrance exams. Students can take the **SAT**, **ACT**, and some may be asked to take the **TOEFL exam**, which is for students whose first language is not English. For more detailed information on college entrance exams check out the **College Planning Timeline for 12th grade**.

Activity	Details
What is the SAT?	**The SAT is a globally recognized college admission exam** that challenges students to show colleges what they know in specific academic areas and how well they can apply that knowledge. It tests a student's knowledge of reading, writing, and math. To prepare for the SAT, your student's high school will offer the PSAT to all students during their 10th or 11th grade, so check with your student's counselor about the date the PSAT will be offered. **Learn more about the SAT by visiting,** https://sat.collegeboard.org/about-tests.
What is the ACT?	**The ACT is an achievement exam,** measuring some of what students learn in school. The ACT has up to five components: English, Mathematics, Reading, Science, and an optional Writing exam. The ACT can be taken instead of the SAT in many cases. Students need to take exams such as the SAT and ACT to qualify to apply to most colleges and universities. **Most students take the SAT or ACT during their junior or senior year of high school.** Most, but not all colleges, require students to take the SAT or ACT as part of their application process. **To learn more about the ACT, visit** the http://www.actstudent.org/.
Do these entrance exams cost money?	Registering for the **SAT exam costs $45 per exam**. Registering for the SAT Subject exam costs $26 for a basic subject exam fee, $26 for language with listening exams, and $20 for all other subject exams. Registering for the **ACT (with no writing section) costs $42.50**. Registering for the **ACT with a writing section costs $58.50**. Registering for the **TOEFL in California costs $185**. **Students may be eligible for a fee waiver.** A fee waiver is a voucher that allows students to avoid paying the exam registration fee. Your student's high school counselor can provide you with a waiver for the SAT, ACT, or TOEFL if you qualify. Fee waivers for exams can cover up to two exams.
How do I sign my student up for these exams?	If your student has decided to take the SAT, s/he must register before the appropriate SAT registration deadline. Students must have an account on College Board to register. **They can go to** http://sat.collegeboard.org/home **to create an account, sign in, and register for SAT exams.** If your student has decided to take the ACT, s/he must register before the appropriate ACT registration deadline. The easiest way to register is for students to create an online account. **They can go to** http://www.actstudent.org/regist/ **to create an account, sign in, and register for ACT exams.** **It is encouraged that students register and take these exams in their junior year of high school. If your student is not satisfied with their score, this gives them more time to take an exam again.**

12TH GRADE

COLLEGE PLANNING ACTIVITIES	
Activity	**Details**
When does my student need to apply to college?	Most students apply for college in the fall of their senior year of high school. See below for more information!
What are the main deadlines for college applications?	**Students who apply to the UC and CSU, submit their applications for admission by November 30th of their senior year.** Application results for UC and CSU normally arrive in March and April. Students have until May 1st to accept or decline college offers. Private, independent colleges, and out-of-state public universities have their own specific deadlines—your student can go to the websites of private, independent colleges, and out-of-state public universities to find out their deadlines. **DEADLINE: For the CSU and UC, high school students must apply by November 30th of their senior year.**
Does it cost money to apply for college?	Yes, most campuses have an application fee that must be submitted at the same time your student submits his/her application. However, the application fee, just like college tuition, varies from campus to campus. • **California Community College—There is no application fee** associated with the California Community College admissions application. • **California State University (CSU)—A $55 application fee** is required for each application. This fee is non-refundable and non-transferable and subject to change. If your student applies online, s/he can pay the application fee by credit or debit card during the application process. If your student is unable to pay by credit or debit card, s/he can send a check or money order to the campus. Though it's recommended to apply online, students who do file using the paper application, should be sure to include a check or money order with their application. • **University of California (UC)—The $70 application fee** entitles your student to apply to one UC campus. If your student applies to more than one campus, s/he must pay an additional $70 for each campus selected. These fees are non-refundable and are subject to change. • **Private/Independent and out-of-state colleges—Independent college, and out-of-state college application fees vary from $0 to $70 or more.** Visit the "Application/Admissions" section of each college your student is applying to in order to confirm the cost of applying and to confirm the process for requesting a fee waiver. Students can also talk to their counselor about fee waivers. **At most of the campuses that have an application fee, students may qualify for a fee waiver, so make sure to check with each campus!**

Activity	Details
After your student submits his or her application, be sure they send all necessary documentation to each campus.	Be sure to send final high school transcripts, test scores, and any additional items that may be in your student's "to-do" list in their student portal.
What if my student's acceptance was provisional? What does that mean?	Read your student's Provisional Admissions Contract for the school s/he was admitted to. It is important your student meets all requirements, or s/he is in danger of having his/her admissions revoked if the conditions are not met.

FINANCIAL AID PLANNING ACTIVITIES

Activity	Details
What are the costs of going to college?	**The biggest costs to attend college are tuition and fees.** Tuition is the amount of money it costs to attend classes at a college or university. Public institutions, like UC, CSU, and CCC, have in-state tuition for residents of California, which sometimes makes attending more affordable. Private, independent colleges charge the same tuition for all students, and each independent institution has its own tuition amount.

Fees are additional mandatory costs that help to cover college activities and benefits afforded to students.

The full cost of a college education includes other things like room and board, health insurance, textbooks and school supplies, travel, and other living expenses. Colleges and universities typically estimate these costs for prospective students, depending on your student's living situation (for example: living on-campus, off-campus, or with parents or relatives).

Chart 1. Resident vs. Non-Resident Tuition at California Public Colleges and Universities |

Tuition	California Community College (CCC)	California State University (CSU)	University of California (UC)
Resident Tuition*	$1,104	$5,472	$12,192
Non-Resident Tuition*	$3,360–$9,600	$14,400	$35,070

For the **non-profit independent colleges in California,** you will need to review the costs for each individual campus. **For additional information about these colleges, please visit http://www.aiccu.edu/member-colleges/.**

Activity	Details
What are the different types of financial aid available to help my student go to college?	Financial aid consists of four different types of aid: • **Loans:** borrowed money for college or career school; you must repay your loans, with interest. • **Grants (Federal and State):** financial aid that doesn't have to be repaid (unless, for example, you withdraw from school and owe a refund). • **Work-study:** a work program through which you earn money to help you pay for school. • **Scholarships:** money awarded to students based on academic or other achievements to help pay for education expenses. Scholarships generally do not have to be repaid. **To learn more about the different types of financial aid, visit** https://studentaid.ed.gov/sa/types.
Are there special circumstances that may provide additional financial aid?	Colleges know that students are unique and each has their own story, background, and family circumstances. There are sometimes additional opportunities for financial aid for students who meet specific criteria. There are also special programs available if your student is: • A foster youth. **For additional information, please visit** http://www.fosteryouthhelp.ca.gov/. • Pursuing a teaching career. **For more information, visit** https://www.teachforamerica.org/. • A veteran or the dependent of one. **For more information, visit** http://www.va.gov/opa/publications/benefits_book.asp There are also special programs available if your student meets either of these criteria. Talk to your students' colleges to learn more about their specific programs. • A law enforcement officer, firefighter, or the dependent of one. • Pursuing the field of child development.
What is the financial aid application known as the FAFSA?	**The Free Application for Federal Student Aid (FAFSA) is the key that opens the door to financial aid.** It is the application students must complete to get financial aid from federal and state programs and from colleges and universities. Even if you or your student are not sure that you will need financial aid to pay for college, we recommend completing the FAFSA anyway. It's free! **Your student can submit the FAFSA as early as October 1st of his/her senior year of high school to make sure s/he meets college and state deadlines.** In most cases, parents also need to complete forms for their students to apply for financial aid. **The quickest and most accurate way to file the FAFSA is online at** https://fafsa.ed.gov/. **Note, this is the only official FAFSA website. Do not submit information to any other websites.** *Continued*

Activity	Details
	DEADLINE: The deadline is March 2nd of your student's senior year, but the earlier you submit it, the better.
	If your student is an **undocumented student,** do not file the FAFSA. If your student has a Social Security number issued by DACA, s/he does not file the FAFSA. Instead, please refer to the question **What is the California Dream Act application?**
What information is needed to file the FAFSA?	If your student is a dependent, then you will need to complete the Free Application for Federal Student Aid (FAFSA). If you utilize an ITIN number for tax-filing purposes, please insert all zeros on the FAFSA as a Social Security number.
	Visit the Student Aid website to learn the difference between "dependent" and "independent." https://studentaid.ed.gov/fafsa/filling-out/.
	In preparation for completing the FAFSA, your student will need the following information readily available. If your student is a dependent student, you (the parent/legal guardian) will also need the following information readily available:
	• **Social Security** number. **Alien Registration** number (only for student, if available and if not a U.S. citizen). • Parent's most recent **federal income tax returns**, **W-2 forms**, and other records of money earned. If your dependent student makes a certain amount of money per year, s/he also needs to provide federal income tax returns, W-2 forms, and other records of money earned. Talk with a tax professional to find out if your student needs to file income tax returns. • Bank statements and records of investments (if applicable). • Records of untaxed income (if applicable). • A **Federal Student Aid ID (FSA ID)** to sign electronically (**if you do not already have one, visit** https://fsaid.ed.gov/npas/index.htm **to obtain one). BOTH you and your student need a PIN to submit the FAFSA.**
	If your student is an **undocumented student,** do not file the FAFSA. If your student has a Social Security number issued by DACA, s/he does not file the FAFSA. Instead, please refer to the question **What is the California Dream Act application?**
Where do I go if I have questions about the FAFSA and federal financial aid?	It's very common for students and parents to have a lot of questions about financial aid and the FAFSA. You can always go to the official website for federal financial aid information, https://studentaid.ed.gov/ to find answers to your questions.

Activity	Details
Why is the FAFSA asking my son to register for selective service?	Registration for the Selective Service is the law for MALES living in the U.S. Male non-citizens living in the U.S. who are 18 through 25 must register to remain eligible for citizenship. Male students who do not register for the Selective Service are subject to being denied federal services. Failure to register will cause ineligibility for a number of federal and state benefits including: • **Federal jobs:** A man must be registered to be eligible for jobs in the Executive Branch of the Federal government and the U.S. Postal Service. This applies only to men born after December 31, 1959. • **Financial aid:** Men who are not registered with Selective Service cannot obtain Federal student loans or grants. This includes Pell Grants, College Work Study, Guaranteed Student/Plus Loans, and National Direct Student Loans. • **Citizenship:** The U.S. Immigration and Naturalization Service (INS) makes registration with Selective Service a condition for U.S. citizenship, if the man first arrived in the U.S. before his 26th birthday and was required to register. • **Federal job training:** The Workforce Investment Act (formerly JTPA) offers important job-training opportunities. This program is only open to those men who register with Selective Service. • **State jobs, loans, and training:** Most states have added additional penalties for those who fail to register with Selective Service. The maximum penalty for failing to register with Selective Service is a $250,000 fine and up to five years in prison.
What is the California Dream Act application?	**Students who are undocumented and who meet AB 540 criteria are eligible to receive state financial aid for their college education.** They must fill out the California Dream Act application, which is the financial aid application for AB 540 eligible students. Complete application instructions and the Dream Act application are online at https://dream.csac.ca.gov/. Even if you or your student are not sure that you will need financial aid to pay for college, we recommend completing the California Dream Act application anyway. It's free! **DEADLINE: The California Dream Act application is due March 2nd, with the same deadline every year. Don't wait until the last minute and risk missing the deadline. Completing this form can be tricky and allowing yourself enough time to complete it is a good tip.**

Activity	Details
How do I know if my student is eligible for the California Dream Act?	If your student is an undocumented student, s/he may qualify for in-state tuition rates at University of California (UC), California State University (CSU), and California Community College campuses and save thousands of dollars. Law AB 540 authorizes undocumented students who meet specified criteria to pay in-state tuition at California public colleges and universities. Students qualify if: • They have attended a California high school for 3 or more years. • They have or will have graduated from a California high school or have attained a GED. • They have registered at or are currently enrolled at an accredited institution of higher education in California. • They have filed or will file an affidavit as required by individual institutions, stating that you will apply for legal residency as soon as possible. (The affidavit will be kept by the college and remain confidential.) **If your student filed an application for permanent residency one year before enrolling in college, s/he may already be eligible for the lower in-state tuition costs to receive California state aid. For more information on financial aid for undocumented students, visit** http://ab540.com/Paying-for-College.html or http://e4fc.org/.
What is the CSS Financial Aid PROFILE?	The **CSS/Financial Aid PROFILE,** http://student.collegeboard.org/css-financial-aid-profile, is an online application that collects information used by certain colleges and scholarship programs to be eligible for institutional aid funds. Some colleges will require this form and additional information, such as tax returns or an institutional application. Your student can file the CSS/Financial Aid PROFILE as early as October 1st of his/her senior year of high school, but should submit it no later than two weeks before the earliest priority filing date as specified by colleges or programs. Visit https://profileonline.collegeboard.org/prf/PXRemotePartInstitutionServlet/PXRemotePartInstitutionServlet.srv to view a list of colleges that use the PROFILE as part of their financial aid process, and see if any of the colleges your student is applying to are on the list. Students are encouraged to call the admissions offices of colleges they are applying to confirm if the college requires the CSS/Financial Aid PROFILE. There is a fee to complete the CSS/Financial Aid PROFILE: $25 for the first college or program to receive your information, and $16 for each additional college or program.

Activity	Details
What is Cal Grant?	**A Cal Grant is money for college you don't have to pay back.** To qualify, you must meet the eligibility and financial requirements as well as any minimum GPA requirements. Cal Grants can be used at any University of California, California State University, or California Community College, as well as qualifying independent and career colleges or technical schools in California. Students who file the FAFSA or the California Dream Act Application should also review their eligibility for a Cal Grant and apply! **For more information on Cal Grant, visit** http://www.csac.ca.gov/.
How does my student apply for Cal Grant?	All California public and charter schools are required to submit your student's GPA, as this is the "application" for Cal Grant. Your student's high school will submit what is called the Cal Grant GPA Verification Form on your student's behalf by or **before March 2nd of the senior year of high school.** **Encourage your student to talk to his/her counselor to confirm the GPA verification paperwork is sent. Your student's Cal Grant application is incomplete without it!**
I know that grants are free money, but what about loans?	Loans are serious business. You and your student need to consider how much you are willing to borrow and whether you or your student will be able to afford to pay back those loans. Loans must be paid after your student leaves school, whether or not s/he graduates. Just because the college has offered your student loans does not require your student to accept those loans, or to accept the full amount of the loans offered. **If your student has applied to and received scholarships, that money should offset your need to accept all the loans your student is offered.**

PREPARING FOR YOUR STUDENT'S FIRST SEMESTER IN COLLEGE

Activity	Details
What is priority registration?	**Priority registration in community college** is the ability for students to register on an earlier date compared to most students. This usually guarantees a space in a course that has limited space. Students are automatically qualified for Priority Registration if they meet one of the following criteria: • Former and current foster youth. • Active duty military and recent veterans. Students can also qualify for Priority Registration if they meet all of the following criteria: • In Extended Opportunity Programs & Services or Disabled Students Programs & Services. • Completed orientation and assessment. • Have an education plan.

Activity	Details
Make sure your student registers for classes	Your student must register for his/her college classes prior to the start of the fall semester. Each college has a different registration process. Your student will receive information from his/her college with directions on registering. If you or your student have any questions about registering for classes, contact your student's college admission office immediately.
Make sure your student prepares for and takes placement exams	Many colleges use placement exams to test students' skills in subjects like math and English to "place" students in the appropriate classes. • **CCC:** Many community colleges use the Accuplacer, http://accuplacer.collegeboard.org/students, which tests students' skills in math, reading, and writing. • **CSU:** The CSU requires students to take the English Placement exam (EPT) and the Entry Level Mathematics (ELM) exam prior to enrollment. However, students may be exempt by means of scores earned on other exams such as the CSU's Early Assessment Program (EAP) exams in English and Mathematics, the SAT, ACT, or Advanced Placement (AP) exams. The EPT and the ELM are not admission exams; instead, they are placement exams. If your student is required to take the EPT and the ELM, but fails to do so, s/he will not be allowed to register for General Education courses at the CSU. • **UC:** ALL students who will enter the University of California (UC) as freshmen must demonstrate their command of the English language by fulfilling the Entry Level Writing Requirement. If your student does not meet the requirement with his/her SAT scores or completed coursework, your student must take the Analytical Writing Placement Examination. **If your student is attending a private, independent school or a school outside of California, s/he may need to fulfill certain placement exam requirements. Visit your student's college's website to learn more!**
What do I need to know about college orientation?	Orientation is an important opportunity that your student should not miss! Every new student is expected to participate in his/her college's orientation. Students will learn how to navigate campus and academic resources, and network with other students, staff, and faculty. **With your student, learn about the different orientation sessions offered at their college/university by visiting your student's school's website or by contacting his/her school.**

Activity	Details
Encourage your student to enroll in a summer program if available at his/ her campus	Summer programs can help your student become familiar with his/her college campus or to college life, something that benefits him/her and prepares your student for his/her first semester/quarter in college. Summer programs can be available for different students of different backgrounds and interests. Some are for students pursuing specific majors, such as STEM (science, technology, engineering, and math). These can be one week long to two months long and may offer the opportunity to take some classes early. **Check your student's college website to learn more about programs that may be available in the summer before his/her freshman year.**
Should my student live on campus or at home?	There are benefits and drawbacks for your student whether s/he lives at home or lives on his/her college campus. When your student lives at home during college, you or your student will not have to spend money on rent, utilities, or other housing expenses. But it may also mean that students don't get the privacy s/he needs to study, or the free time to devote to his/her studies and other pursuits during college. Living on-campus (dorms) or off-campus (apartments) housing will help your student learn all the things that are not taught in the classroom. **Have an honest conversation with your student about what it means to be a commuter student living at home, and how you can help him/her be the best student possible. If your student is going to live on- or off-campus, talk to your student about reasonable expectations of how they will need to manage his/her time as a student, and how that will impact any responsibilities at home.**
When is my student's first payment due?	Once your student registers for college, s/he will begin to get important information from the college, such as an online academic account and an online financial aid account. Make sure your student learns to log in to these regularly to stay on top of his/her academics and finances. Your student's financial aid account should give him/her the following information: • The total balance due for upcoming term and the deadline. • The amount available through the various sources of aid that will be applied to that balance. **If they have questions about their account, encourage them to visit the financial aid office on campus.**

Activity	Details
Make a note of all important deadlines related to your student's financial aid	You or your student should put important financial aid related deadlines into your personal calendars. These deadlines include: • When college payments are due each term (usually before the beginning of the term). • When financial aid comes through to his/her student account (such as loans released to you or when scholarship money comes in). • When applications are due for any renewable scholarships.
Submit any documents requested by the office of financial aid	The office of financial aid will often contact your student to submit the following: • Copy of your student's tax return or your tax return. • Supplemental forms. • Dependent/independent verification form. **Be sure to ask your child to check his/her student accounts/portals to confirm the documents being requested of him/her.**
Have your student open a checking account	If your student does not have a checking account, be sure to have them open one before they start college. While there are many benefits to having a bank account, most colleges will refund their financial aid money to a bank account on file. If the student does not have a bank account, a paper check will be issued which takes a lot more time. **If your student is unable to open a checking account, contact the financial aid office at his/her school for alternative options.**

WEEKLY TIME LOG

	Sunday	Monday	Tuesday	Wednesday	Thursday	Friday	Saturday
7:00–8:00							
8:00–9:00							
9:00–10:00							
10:00–11:00							
11:00–12:00							
12:00-1:00							
1:00–2:00							
2:00–3:00							
3:00–4:00							
4:00–5:00							
5:00–6:00							
6:00–7:00							
7:00–8:00							
8:00–9:00							
9:00–10:00							
10:00–11:00							
11:00–12:00							
12:00-1:00							
1:00–2:00							
2:00–3:00							
3:00–4:00							
4:00–5:00							
5:00–6:00							
6:00–7:00							

Academic Majors and the Holland Code
Realistic	Agricultural Management, Agriculture Agronomy, Animal Science, Architectural Drafting, Automotive Services, Aviation, Ecology, Electronics Engineering (Aerospace, Biomedical, Chemical, Civil, Electrical, Industrial, Mechanical Facilities), Management Fire, Science Fish & Wildlife Management, Forestry Heating, Air Conditioning, Horticulture, Industrial Arts, Landscape Architecture, Law Enforcement, Medical Technology, Military Science, Natural Resources, Physical Fitness, and Physiology Welding.
Investigative	Anthropology, Archeology, Astronomy, Biochemistry, Biological Science, Botany, Chemistry, Computer Information Systems, Computer Science, Criminal Justice, Economics, Food Science, Genetics, Geography, Geology, Health Science (Pre-dental, Pre-medicine, Pre-optometry, Pre-pharmacy, Pre-Physical Therapy, Pre-Veterinary Medicine), Mathematics, Medical Lab Technician, Meteorology, Paramedics, Physical Sciences, Physics, Psychology, Science Education, Social Sciences, Sociology, and Zoology.
Artistic	Advertising, Architecture, Art Education, Art History, Broadcasting, Cinematography, Classics, Comparative Languages, Creative Writing, Dance, Design (Advertising Design, Fashion/Textile, Costume Design, Crafts & Design, Graphic Design, Interior Design, Industrial Design), English, Foreign Languages, Fashion Merchandising, Fine Arts (Drama, Music, Musicology, Studio Arts), Humanities, Journalism, Linguistics, Mass Communications, Medical Illustration, Music Education, Philosophy, Photography, and Theater Arts.
Social	Child Development, Counseling, Criminology, Dietetics & Nutrition, Education (Ed. Administration, Elementary, Early Childhood, ESL, Foreign Language, Health, Physical Education, Secondary Education, Social Science Education, Special Education), Ethnic Studies, Family Studies, Hearing and Speech, Home Economics, Human Services, Occupational Therapy, Nursing, Park Administration, Public Health, Recreation, Religious Studies, Respiratory Care, Social Welfare, Sports Administration, Substance Abuse Counseling, Urban Studies, and Women's Studies.
Enterprising	Business Administration, Business Education, Consumer Economics, Cosmetology, Culinary Training, Finance, Government, History, Hotel Management, Hospitality, Housing, Human Resources, Information Systems, Insurance, International Relations, Management, Marketing, Personnel and Labor Relations, Political Science, Pre-law, Production Management, Public Administration, Public Relations, Real Estate, Restaurant Management, Retail Merchandising, Transportation Travel & Tourism.
Conventional	Accounting, Banking and Financial, Bookkeeping, Business Education, Computer Operations, Computer Programming, Court Reporting, Data Management, Dental Hygiene, Financial Planning, Food Service Management, Industrial Education, Mathematics Education, Medical Administration, Office Systems, Paralegal Studies, Purchasing/Materials Management, Secretarial Procedures, Small Business Operations, and Statistics.
Copyright © 2016 by Santa Cruz County Regional Occupational Program. Reprinted by permission.

SENIOR YEAR COLLEGE/FINANCIAL AID CHECKLIST

At any point - ask for help

- ☐ From your high school counselor
- ☐ From College OPTIONS **(530) 244-4022**
- ☐ From the college you applied to; don't hesitate to call the Admissions, Financial Aid or Housing office—they want to help!

September

- ❏ Attend the Financial Aid Information Night at your school. (check with your counselor for your school's date) **www.collegeoptions.org**
- ☐ Attend a Cash for College workshop (check with your counselor for your school's date) for free help completing the FAFSA or the CA DREAM Application. **www.calgrants.org**
- ☐ Estimate your Expected Family Contribution **www.tinyurl.com/myefc**
- ☐ US Citizens and eligible non-citizens: Complete the FAFSA on the Web Worksheet, at **www.fafsa.gov** You and one of your parents should each create a Federal Student Aid ID so you can e-sign the FAFSA for faster processing. **https://fsaid.ed.gov**
- ☐ DREAM Application worksheet at **www.caldreamact.org**
- ☐ Create a personalized electronic or paper calendar of deadlines for college admission and financial aid applications.
- ☐ Start drafting essays for college and scholarship applications.
- ☐ Sign up for the SAT and/or ACT (**www.sat.collegeboard.com** or **www.actstudent.org**) if you haven't taken them.
- ☐ Memorize your Social Security number. If you do not have a Social Security number, talk to your counselor.

- ☐ Apply for a driver's license or state ID card if you don't already have one. You may need one for financial aid verification purposes.
- ☐ Research career options thoroughly; the better informed you are, the more effective your college search will be. **www.onetonline.org**
- ☐ Research colleges online. **www.usnews.com/education**
- ☐ Attend local college fairs and meet college representatives visiting your school.
- ☐ Ask teachers, counselors, employers, and/ or coaches for letters of recommendation (at least 2 weeks before a deadline).
- ☐ Your e-mail address should be appropriate for communicating with colleges, lenders & employers. Example: firstnamelastname@ _____.com

October

- ☐ **Oct 1:** FAFSA and CA Dream Applications are available online (**www.fafsa.gov** or **www.caldreamact.org**). Submit the appropriate application as early as possible. **Be sure and use the DRT (Data Retrieval Tool) from FAFSA to report your reported income from the IRS. Provide required e-signatures and email address for faster processing.** Due March 2 if you want to be considered for Cal Grant.
- ☐ The College Board's CSS PROFILE is an additional financial aid application that some private colleges require. Research if you need to complete this application. **profileonline.collegeboard.org**
- ☐ **Oct 1** CSU & UC applications available. Check other colleges for app availability.
- ☐ Visit colleges or take a virtual tour online.
- ☐ Planning to live on-campus? Research what your potential colleges' housing application processes are; some have application deadlines as early as October.

November

- ☐ **Nov 30** CSU & UC applications due. Check other colleges for deadlines. Priority application deadline for CSU campuses' Educational Opportunity Program (EOP).
- ☐ Start researching and applying for scholarships. Some have early deadlines.
- ☐ Review your FAFSA Student Aid Report and make corrections at **www.fafsa.gov** if necessary. If you don't receive your report within three weeks of submitting your FAFSA, call toll free 800-433-3243.

December

- ☐ Confirm official SAT/ACT scores were sent to colleges.
- ☐ Apply for scholarships at the colleges you have applied to; some deadlines are as early as December.

January

- ☐ Check your online portal at each college you applied to and your email on a **weekly basis**. Respond to colleges' requests for information promptly.
- ☐ Ask your counselor how your high school submits seniors' Cal Grant GPA (paper forms or electronic upload). If paper, fill out a paper Cal Grant GPA Verification form and turn it in to your counseling office by March 2nd. **www.calgrants.org**
- ☐ Keep a copy of everything you submit (paper or electronic copy).
- ☐ Watch for application confirmation emails from your college(s); create a "portal" for each college you applied to. Monitor each portal for admissions decisions.
- ☐ Apply for scholarships!

February

- ☐ Manage your Cal Grant status online using WebGrants for Students at **www.webgrants4students.org**

SENIOR YEAR COLLEGE/FINANCIAL AID CHECKLIST

☐ Math and English assessment tests: check each college you applied to. Do you need to take these tests? You may be able to waive these assessments through SAT, ACT or AP exam scores.

☐ Apply for scholarships!

March

☐ **March 2** is the Cal Grant deadline to submit the FAFSA (or CA DREAM Application for AB540 students).

☐ Watch for college acceptance letters and financial aid offers via email and your college portal(s).

☐ Manage your Cal Grant. Look for email messages from the California Student Aid Commission and check your status. **www.webgrants4students.org**

☐ Planning to attend a community college? Apply, take assessment tests, send in your high school transcripts, and sign up for an orientation. Apply for EOPS & SSS.

☐ Apply for scholarships!

April

☐ Watch for college acceptance letters and financial aid offers via email and your college portal(s).

☐ Evaluate all financial aid offers carefully. Ask questions! All offer letters are *estimates* until finalized tax information is reflected on your FAFSA or CA DREAM Application.

☐ Utilize College OPTIONS' Cost of Attendance Comparison Worksheet to determine your actual "net" cost at each college you are considering. Carefully examine your and your family's budget and "cash flow." Can you afford your intended college for the 4-5 years you will be attending? **www.collegeoptions.org** (look at the Financial Aid section)

☐ Consider grants, work-study and other aid (scholarships) you don't have to repay before accepting a student loan.

☐ Notify the financial aid offices at all your possible colleges of any scholarships received that are not on your award letter. Ask them how these changes will affect your award letter from them. You may need to rethink your school choice.

☐ If you are short of funds necessary to pay mandatory deposits to the college (e.g. tuition, dorms, meal plans, etc.), ask the college if you can defer deposits and/or make payments on an installment plan.

☐ Use your college portal to accept and/or decline your financial aid awards.

☐ Manage your Cal Grant status using WebGrants for Students at **www.webgrants4students.org** If you do not have any information available on the "Award Detail" tab by mid-April, call toll free 888-224-7268 and ask them to help you determine your status.

☐ Make sure you have fulfilled any financial aid verification requests from your college's financial aid office. If you're unsure if you have any requirements, check your portal or contact the financial aid office.

☐ Apply for scholarships!

May

☐ **May 1** is the deadline to notify the four-year college that you plan to attend. Use your college portal to accept your offer of admission (you might have to make an enrollment deposit and/or register for orientation by May 1 as well).

☐ Look for a summer job, sign up for a summer class at the community college or volunteer with a business or organization to help investigate your career interests.

☐ Arrange your college housing plans.

☐ Missed the March 2 Cal Grant deadline? Complete the FAFSA to be considered for federal and institutional aid.

Summer

☐ Confirm your high school graduation and college of attendance. **www.webgrants4students.org**

☐ Keep checking your college portal. Follow through on any "to-do" items.

☐ If you have Special Circumstances due to job loss, death, hardship, divorce, large medical expenses, an unusual family/parental situation, etc., which were not reflected on your financial aid application, contact your college's financial aid office ASAP so they can determine if they can use Professional Judgment to make adjustments to your financial aid award.

☐ Make sure your "master promissory note" is signed for any Federal student loans. **www.studentloans.gov**

☐ Read the fine print on your student loan agreement, especially if the loan is a non-government (alternative) loan. Know your repayment obligations while you are in school as well as after you graduate.

☐ Financial aid "disbursements" (distribution of the funds) typically come after the semester/quarter starts. If you are unable to afford any costs that will come due before aid disbursements, communicate with your college's financial aid office.

☐ Four-year college-bound students: Attend your college's orientation.

☐ Register for classes.

☐ Claim scholarships you won. You may need to turn in copies of your fall class schedule (or some other proof of enrollment). Check with each scholarship provider.

Apply for financial aid and scholarships every year you are in college.

Revised 8-17-2017

COST OF ATTENDANCE COMPARISON WORKSHEET

	Community College	California State University	University College	Private	Trade
Tuition and Fees	$	$	$	$	$
Room	$	$	$	$	$
Board	$	$	$	$	$
Books & Supplies	$	$	$	$	$
Computer Costs	$	$	$	$	$
Transportation	$	$	$	$	$
Personal:					
Clothing	$	$	$	$	$
Laundry	$	$	$	$	$
Medical	$	$	$	$	$
Entertainment	$	$	$	$	$
Other	$	$	$	$	$
Total COA	$	$	$	$	$

college OPTIONS

Decision Tool	Individual Campus Factors to Consider (factors that matter to YOU)	Reputation of Academics/ Accreditation	Majors that interest you	Cost	Size of campus (does it "fit" you?)	Social Activities/ Environment	Availability of Housing (Dorms, Apartments)	Sports (playing or attending events)	Distance from home	Note: Each factor is created by you.
	Assign a weight to that factor (between 1-10)	10	10	10	8	6	6	5	3	Total Rating Points
Campuses being considered.	Name of college: **College #1**									
	Score:	8	3	5	8	3	5	3	2	
	Rating Points:	80	30	50	64	18	30	15	6	**293**
For each campus, assign a score to each factor.	Name of college: **College #2**									
	Score:	6	8	6	6	6	9	8	3	
	Rating Points:	60	80	60	48	36	54	40	9	**387**
Multiply the score by that factor's weight to find the "rating points" for that factor.	Name of college:									
	Score:									
	Rating Points:									
	Name of college:									
	Score:									
	Rating Points:									
Total the rating points for that campus and write the total in the far right column.	Name of college:									
	Score:									
	Rating Points:									
	Name of college:									
	Score:									
	Rating Points:									
	Name of college:									
	Score:									
	Rating Points:									

www.ingramcontent.com/pod-product-compliance
Lightning Source LLC
Chambersburg PA
CBHW051409200326
41520CB00023B/7168